# RES3T

## 8 PRINCIPLES GUARANTEED TO CHANGE YOUR MINDSET IN ORDER TO CHANGE YOUR LIFE

# JEFF COATS

Paperback ISBN: 978-0-692-15507-3

Cover Design: Daniel Ojedokun, Officialdannymedia@gmail.com

Editing and Interior Layout: Jeff Coats, Suzanne Potts, and Jeff Braucher (santafeworddoctor.com)

This book is dedicated to the many people who have had struggles in their lives yet have pulled themselves together to live their best lives and beat all the odds against them!

This book is in loving memory of my mom:
Terri Lynn Coats

# #LOVEFREEDOM

A dim hope turns into a bright future.

I received a
20 year adult
prison sentence
at 14 years old

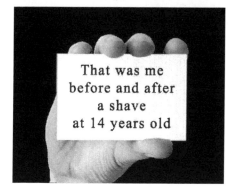

That was me
before and after
a shave
at 14 years old

(Real Friends
not
Facebook Friends)

During my sentence
1 friend
stayed in touch
with me

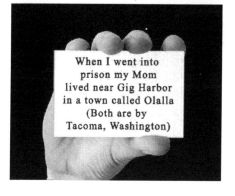

When I went into
prison my Mom
lived near Gig Harbor
in a town called Olalla
(Both are by
Tacoma, Washington)

That event was the
second event that
changed my life

Which has led me
to where I am
in this moment
showing you this

When I first released
I worked for a
Mortgage company
as an
IT Administrator

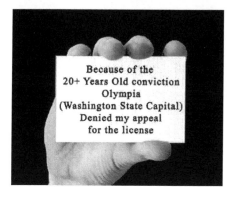

I also speak to the
Washington State
Legislature

To raise awareness
and to inspire our politicians
for real change in our
judicial system

The other thing I do today is:

I am a licensed Real Estate Agent with Keller Williams

Despite the journey to get to this point in my life, I live my life today with a smile and with a heart of compassion and the desire to inspire!

# Contents

# Introduction

# My Story

*"The meaning of life is to find your gift.*

*The purpose of life is to give it away."*

*~ Pablo Picasso ~*

Whether you're successful but unsatisfied, or at rock bottom, you can make choices right now to change your circumstances. I want to inspire you to believe in yourself, to believe in possibility, and to understand that there are concrete steps you can take to keep you moving forward in the direction of your goals and dreams.

I'm introducing the Dedicated 8—eight principles that have provided the guidance and inspiration I've needed to get through really tough times. They've helped me discover my path and find my way back when I've gone off

1

course. I'm sharing the Dedicated 8 because they work. I'm not promising instant success; changing the course of your life is not always easy. It is a path that requires dedication, effort, willpower, humility, and love. Love for yourself, love for life, and love for the truth.

I was incarcerated at the age of 14 and sent to adult prison. As of this writing, I was incarcerated for 17 out of my 38 years on this planet, almost half my life. You might be thinking, "Okay, this guy has obviously been through a lot, but how can he help me? I haven't been in prison. And how can he know anything about living out in the real world?" Fair questions. All I can say is that for as long as I can remember, I have had a natural ability to connect with people—people of all ages and from all walks of life. I had this ability before I went to prison, and developed my natural empathy and honed my communication skills while in prison.

After being released from prison in 2011, I had the opportunity to put my ability to connect with people to the test. I was entering a very different world from the one I'd left in 1994—not as a little boy but as a grown man who would be required to make a living and support himself. I was also aware that if I wanted to experience the fullness of life, I'd have to figure out, and fast, how to create lasting relationships that weren't determined by proximity and confinement, or limited by time.

In the last several years, in conjunction with my work as a successful real estate broker, I've been giving motivational talks around the country—at colleges and universities, in prisons and juvenile detention centers, to youth groups and Realtors, at entrepreneurial events and nonprofit organizations, to families, and, whether they like it or not, to my own friends. In this context I've had the opportunity to share my Dedicated 8 Principles. After I step away from the podium or finish a talk, I'm often approached by individuals who wish to share their own stories. After they share with me, they frequently ask me to elaborate on my Principles. They want to understand what it takes to accept difficult situations and how to cope with their painful circumstances. Or they have great lives but feel deep down in their bodies that a change is needed, and are looking for clues about how to create that change. More than anything, they want to know what it takes to move forward and how they can reach their goals.

My answers to these questions and more are in this book.

***

I was born in 1980 and grew up poor in a small town called Olalla in Washington State. We were so poor we had to use large containers for catching rainwater and snow so we had water to drink, bathe in, and use for doing the dishes and washing our clothes by hand. For a time, my mom, stepdad, brother, and I lived in a shack made of four 4 ft. x 8 ft. pieces of particle board. It had a little fire pit in the middle that separated where my parents slept from where my younger brother, Bill, and I slept. A blanket hung over the "entrance," hiding our view of what would one day be the trailer we'd live in. We weren't able to live in it until we could afford power and heat. It was an aluminum trailer, and without heat we would have frozen to death.

My mother and stepdad relied on the state for assistance. Neither of them had jobs. Just habits. Horrible habits. Both were alcoholics and drug addicts. To pick up extra money during the winter, my mom would make Christmas door wreaths. My stepdad would occasionally get work repairing motorcycles. However, whatever they earned, more often than not, went for alcohol and drugs, not food, utilities, or clothing.

One night right before Columbus Day in 1991 when I was 11 years old, I was washing the dishes like I did every night. I was standing at the sink in our trailer, looking out the window, watching the rain pour down outside. My stepdad, my mom, and her girlfriend were drinking and doing drugs right behind me at the kitchen table. My brother was in the living room (if you could call it that) watching TV.

I was zoning out, watching the rain drops hit the kitchen window while I washed. I was standing on one leg with the ball of my right foot propped on my left knee, kind of like a dancer. Suddenly I got smacked on the back of my head, and my mom's friend snarled, "Put your foot down!" So I put my foot down and kept doing the dishes. I was vaguely aware that she was still hovering over me, but after washing dishes for a while, I relaxed back into my zone and eventually put my foot back up on my knee. She hit me again and suggested to my stepdad that a willow branch would teach me to listen and not to forget.

They all started laughing and my stepdad said, "Yeah, go get a willow branch. I'll teach you a lesson about listening." I went outside in the pouring rain and walked to the willow tree. I reasoned that if I got a small, skinny branch, it would hurt less. (I had no idea that a skinny whip would sting more.) I picked the narrowest branch I could find and brought it inside. My stepdad told me to "assume the position," which meant I had to get into a spread-eagle position against the wall. He proceeded to whip me all over my upper body. I was twisting and turning and screaming. It hurt worse than anything I'd ever felt up to that point in my life.

The elementary school my brother and I went to knew how poor we were—that we didn't have running water or clean clothes. I guess some people in the administration had put the word out and members of the school community donated clothing for us. Every morning, my brother and I would arrive early and shower in the health room at school and then change into donated clothing. On the day after the willow branch beating, I chose a D.A.R.E. (Drug Abuse Resistance Education) sweatshirt that was a little small for me. I wanted to wear it because D.A.R.E. was my favorite class.

At the end of the D.A.R.E. class that day, the police officer who taught it asked me to stay behind to speak with her. She had a strange look in her eyes and asked, "Can you lift up your shirt?" During class I'd raised my hand a few times and apparently my shirt had hiked up far enough to expose the whip marks.

She looked at my wounds and asked, "Do you have chicken pox?"

"No."

"What are these welts?"

"I don't know."

"How did you get them? You have so many."

"I don't know."

After talking to her for quite a while, I finally told her the story of what had happened the night before, and my brother and I were put into foster care that day.

Foster care in Washington State was quite a journey for me. I bounced around a lot because of the structure of the foster care system itself and because I didn't always understand the rules. I was also rebellious and frequently endured abuse at the hands of foster parents. After being in foster care for about two years, I decided I wanted to try living with my parents again. I thought my life would be more stable at my parents' home, and since I'd grown taller and matured a little, I felt I could hold my own against my stepdad.

I'd been back home with my family for a week when my mom told me my stepdad wanted to talk to me. She drove me out to the garage where he was working on a friend's motorcycle. Without looking at me, he said, "I'm going to cut right to the chase...you can't stay with us. It's not because of anything you've done, we just can't afford to feed you, and so it's better if you're in foster homes because they can afford to take care of you."

Because I'd bounced around so much in foster care, I was put in a state-run group home instead. It was a group home that transitioned juvenile offenders from juvenile detention facilities back into homes in the community. In hindsight I realize it was not the best place to put a foster kid. Soon after arriving at the home, I took part in a plan with a couple of older guys to steal a car. I went along with the idea because I thought it would be cool to have a new car to drive to school. It never occurred to me that there would be any problem with the plan or any real consequences.

The plan became real and then took on a life of its own. Here's the short version of the story: We found a man sitting in his BMW in downtown Tacoma and threatened him with a steel pipe concealed in a bag. We drove around Tacoma looking for a secluded place to drop him that was far enough away to prevent him from reporting us in time for the police to catch us.

We drove to a not-so-secluded local river and decided to put him in the trunk of the car while we looked for a more secluded area. I stayed in the car while the two other guys bound his hands and feet with duct tape and covered his mouth with a strip of tape. They shut him in the trunk, but because they'd accidentally covered his nose with the tape, he began to panic and started to kick the inside of the trunk. My friends jumped in the car and told me what had happened. We all agreed we should open the trunk, remove the tape from his mouth and nose, and try to calm him down.

I'd never been in such a fancy car before and discovered, to my amazement, that it had a trunk release button on the key. Thinking that the man would not be able to jump out of the trunk, I pushed the button to open the trunk while all three of us were still sitting in the car. The man had untapped himself while in the trunk and when I pushed the button he jumped out, started running down the street, and managed to hop onto a garbage truck that was driving by. We panicked!—and immediately drove the car back downtown and dropped it at a bus station.

When we got caught I was charged with attempted murder, conspiracy to commit murder, robbery, conspiracy to commit robbery, kidnapping, and conspiracy to commit kidnapping. I was only 14 years old, but the prosecution wanted to try me as an adult.

The year was 1994, and politicians were talking about being tough on juvenile crime because juvenile crime rates were as high as they'd ever been. A political scientist named John Dilulio Jr. was predicting that the rates would spike even higher. He called juvenile criminals superpredators—a new breed of offender with no respect for human life. In 1994 US judges transferred over 13,000 juveniles into the adult system.

The judge in my case ultimately agreed with the prosecution that I could not be rehabilitated, so the State of Washington tried me as an adult. I pleaded guilty to robbery, conspiracy to commit robbery, and conspiracy to commit murder. The plea was considered an Alford plea, meaning I maintained my claim of innocence but understood that the case against me was strong. It was a deal. I got twenty years (the maximum sentence would have been life without parole). If I'd been convicted as a juvenile, I would have gotten around two and a half years in the juvenile system. If you would like to hear an exceptional podcast by Cited about my life and this story, go to **podcast.res3t.com.**

**The Three F's**

When I first entered prison, just after I was released from segregation (solitary confinement) where I'd spent my first 90 days, I was walking around the track out in the yard. It was early in the morning and the only other person outside was a huge white guy doing pull-ups. He was called Big Tom because he was around six-four and 300 pounds. He saw me and called me over to him. I was terrified, but he was friendly and asked me if I had any questions.

"Do people die here?"

"Yeah."

"Do people get stabbed here?"

He nodded.

"Do people get raped here?"

He said, "Listen, you just have to follow the three F's, and you'll be fine."

I thought, *What in the eff are the three F's!!?"*

"If someone's going to disrespect you, you have three options: you're either going to fight them, let them fuck you, or hit the fence [try to escape]. So when that time comes, you'll know it, and you'll make your choice, and when you make that choice, that choice is what's gonna follow you for the rest of your prison sentence."

Just a few months later, a 35-year-old sex offender called me a punk. (*Punk*, a derogatory term in prison, meaning you are a walking victim, someone anyone can do anything to at any time.) He disrespected me; it was my first three-F moment. What was I going to do? Fight, get fucked, or hit the fence? I decided to fight, but the guy was bigger and older than I was, so I tried to kick him down some stairs to get the upper hand.

Unfortunately, he didn't fall down the stairs. He covered his face with his arms and pushed toward me. As he was getting closer, I was backing up and swinging for the fences because I didn't want him to get the upper hand. As I backed up, I kicked over a five-gallon bucket used to catch the overflow water from a fountain in our living area. Water flooded the floor, and I slipped, my head hitting the concrete wall, and then slamming on the cement floor. BAM! I was knocked out and had a seizure.

While I was having the seizure, this guy jumped on top of me and BAM! BAM! BAM! BAM! BAM! hit me in the face five times. He then jumped up and ran to his room. I was taken out on a stretcher and transported to the local

13

hospital. My face was so badly beaten that the guards told the doctors they thought I'd fallen from the third tier. That fight gave me two black eyes for two years.

Word spread around the prison that a 15-year-old had started a fight with a 35-year-old sex offender. That earned me a reputation: I'd fight if anyone tried to take advantage of me. I only got into 15 more fights in the 17 years I was in prison. I lost all of them except the last one, but I never got raped or taken advantage of, and more important, I survived!

The title of this book is *Res3t*. I replaced the *e* with *3* because no matter where you are or who you are, you are going to be confronted with the "3 F's" whenever you enter into a new situation, job, or relationship. Are you going to fight for what you want, or are you going to let someone else take advantage of you, use you, undermine you, or take credit for your work? Are you going to fight for your life, or are you simply going to give up, run away, and attempt to escape from your responsibility to yourself? The choice is yours. I think you can tell where I stand. Fight for yourself and your goals. You are worth it!

# Chapter One

# Dedicated 8

If you're anything like me, you just skipped over the Introduction to get started with this awesome book. Until I started writing my own, I never realized how important the Introduction is. So be sure to read that first before you begin this Dedicated 8 journey. You won't be disappointed!

At various points in my life I've experienced what I call **SPIRIT**, or as Oprah calls it, the "aha! moment." It is an unexpected experience that creates an awakening in consciousness. This awakening changes the course of your life. In my case it was the death of my mother while I was still in prison that shifted my mindset and gave me the impetus to begin reading and studying, which ultimately gave me the tools and information to work in real estate when I was released.

When I first got sentenced to prison and was taken away from the world, I had to **ACCEPT** what was happening to me and where I was. I had little choice. There was nothing to be accomplished by fighting or denying the truth. Once I accepted my reality, I needed to learn to **COPE** with the situation. I had to find constructive ways to occupy my time to keep from going crazy or falling into depression. I then got to a place within myself where I needed to take **RESPONSIBILITY** for what I'd done, for where I was, for who I was, for what I wanted, and for the decisions I would make moving forward. This was the only way for me to clear my conscience enough to be able to focus on what I wanted to achieve once I left prison.

As my release date got closer, I realized I needed to figure out what I'd be doing to support myself when I was out of prison. As I began setting **GOALS**, I became more focused and positive and ready to be a productive member of society. To manifest my goals, I understood that I had to take **ACTION**. While in prison, I did this by taking classes and learning as much as I could about the areas I was interested in. I also knew I would have to take **RISKS** in order to push forward. Once I was released, I took the risk of applying for a job I was not really qualified to do and then telling the truth about my background. I got the job! Finally, I had to **NETWORK** with intention to create a support team to help me get where I wanted to go. I have learned that very little is possible in life without the assistance of other people.

The principles I introduced above are called the Dedicated 8 because you have to be dedicated to them, each one of them, in order to accomplish the goal or goals you have set for yourself.

**SPIRIT** refers to a moment in your life that blows you out of the water, that changes the trajectory of your life, that wakes you up to a different possibility. It can happen at any moment. You cannot create it or control it. I call it Spirit because it is a life-altering experience that calls your spirit into awareness and forces you to look at yourself and your life with different eyes.

**ACCEPTANCE** is a state of being that must be achieved, no matter where you are or what you are doing, before you can make any move forward. If you are constantly chafing against your current situation, always irritated and resisting, you will not have the energy or focus to create a different experience for yourself. Accepting your situation does not mean you have to like it, it means you have to stop resisting and stop denying so you can take stock, realign with what it is you really want to do, and cultivate the energy and skills to move forward.

**COPING** is a strategy to keep you sane, creative, and positive while you figure out what you want and how to get it. You are not necessarily taking action in the direction of your goals at this point, you are simply recharging, getting your bearings, and gearing up for your next move.

**RESPONSIBILITY** – You cannot accomplish anything with ease and grace without a clear conscience and a feeling of empowerment. When you make your amends, absolve, forgive, and own your part in any relationship or situation that has been weighing on your mind, you empower yourself to move forward. Any nagging feeling of guilt or blame holds you back by keeping you tied to the past and burdened by negative feelings of shame and resentment. Free yourself by taking responsibility!

**GOALS** – Setting clear goals will immediately get you halfway there. If you are unsure about what you want or where you want to go, your path will lead you to a dead end or just circle back to the beginning. Be clear, intentional, consistent, and persistent, and you will find you are able to reach goals that might have seemed unattainable in the past.

**ACTION** is both the most obvious and most effective of all the Dedicated 8. You cannot accomplish anything if you are not willing to put energy behind your desire. A desire, goal, dream, or vision without action is just a fantasy. It has no substance and will never become manifest unless you are willing to put your energy behind it.

**RISK** – Calculated risks are necessary if you are ever to achieve anything of significance. You must, at some point in your process, be willing to get out of your comfort zone and risk failing or looking foolish or being rejected or losing, because nothing truly worthwhile comes easily. If it seems easy it's because of all the effort you've put out over the course of your life.

**NETWORKING** – We live in the world with other people and we need them to help us achieve our goals. We need a prospective boss to take a chance on us; we need a friend to connect us to the person who can get us the information we need to create what we want. We need support and encouragement and we need partners. Relationships are everything!

I am using the word FREEDOM as an acronym to help you remember how to employ the Dedicated 8. Freedom reminds me to appreciate my amazing life and all the opportunities available to me. When I was in prison I naturally thought about freedom and what I needed to do before my release so I would be prepared for freedom. Now that I am free, I come back to this word daily in order to make sure I'm moving toward my goals and following the Dedicated 8 to accomplish them. If this program can work for me, it can work for you! (I have not included Spirit because it is an unpredictable quality or experience and largely out of your control. You will know it when you encounter it.)

| | | |
|---|---|---|
| **ACCEPTANCE** | F – | **Focus** on your present Circumstance and feel your **Feelings** |
| **COPING** | R – | **Research, Rest,** and Recreation |
| **RESPONSIBILITY** | E – | Cultivate **Esteem** for yourself by owning your stuff |
| **GOALS** | E – | **Educate** yourself and **Enumerate** your goals |
| **ACTION** | D – | Employ **Discipline** in the **Doing** |
| **RISK** | O – | **Open** yourself to **Opportunity** |
| **NETWORKING** | M – | **Meet Many** people |

# Chapter Two

# Naysayers

*"Whenever we hear an opinion and believe it, we make an*

*agreement, and it becomes part of our belief system."*

~ *Don Miguel Ruiz,* The Four Agreements ~

**Speaking Truth to Power**

When you commit a crime, you are ordered to pay restitution to the victim, to the state, or possibly even to both. If you go to prison with a $5,000 debt, and you're there for 17 years, when you get out, you may wind up owing as much as (or more than) $50,000. While I was inside I discovered there was a process by which I could get in front of a judge and ask the judge to forgive the interest if I had the money to pay the original fine. (Since you don't have an income when you're in prison, it just doesn't make sense for interest to be added to your original debt.)

After I was released I went to the county clerk and got the paperwork. I then asked the clerk to help me fill out the paperwork to get the interest waived from my fines. He said, "That's not going to happen." When I asked why, he said, "The courts just don't do that. They don't get involved. Once it's set, it's set, and interest kicks in and then you have to pay your fine with interest."

I said, "Really? You've never seen the interest waived from a fine before?" He repeated that it just doesn't happen and that it's not going to happen. If I'd listened to this guy, the next part of this story would never have unfolded the way it did.

This guy was a **Naysayer**. He was trying, whether he knew it or not, to discourage me from accomplishing my goal. And, of course, it turned out he was giving me his personal opinion and not the facts. I filed the paperwork anyway and went to the hearing. I brought the money I owed for my original fine and, sure enough, the judge waived the interest.

She then called the county clerk—the one who'd discouraged me—to the courtroom where she said to him, "I'm waiving the interest from this fine."

Visibly upset, the clerk said, "If you waive the interest, this affects everybody."

The judge replied, "Would you rather be paid or not? I think we'd rather be paid. He has the money."

In the end, if I'd listened to the naysayer, I never would have achieved what I have today because I would still be paying off a huge fine to the state right now. But instead, I followed my goal and my gut. I researched the process and believed I was doing the right thing. I figured if it didn't work out, at least I tried and did everything I could to support myself and my dreams.

*"Naysayers have little power over us—*

*unless we give it to them."*

*~ Arianna Huffington ~*

## Naysayers, and the Inner Critic

A naysayer is an individual who discourages you from trying for and reaching your goal. This individual can be anyone—it can even be you if you are the one who is telling yourself you cannot achieve your goal. More often than not, the naysayer (or hater) is obvious. The naysayer offers (often unsolicited) negative or discouraging comments. However, sometimes a naysayer can masquerade as a positive person giving words of "encouragement." For instance, when I decided only several months out of prison to interview for a processor job in a mortgage company (as described in chapter nine), my aunt "encouraged" me to try for a job at a fast-food restaurant instead because I'd worked briefly in a restaurant when I first got out of prison on work release several months before I moved in with her.

Encountering the naysayer, or finding that you are playing that role with yourself, can happen anytime during your journey toward your goal. In the beginning, after you've determined you want to change your life circumstance, but before you've decided exactly what you want to do next, you may encounter many of the "positive" naysayers, people who say they have your best interest in mind but caution you to stay "safe," to try not to reach too far above your station. Sometimes these individuals can even be your family members. They may encourage you to keep the job you don't like, or simply tell you how unattainable your plans are even before you've had the chance to completely think things through and develop them. Just be mindful of these people and try to understand their perspective and heart. However, stay focused on your path and *believe* in it and yourself!

When you encounter naysayers, take a sidestep around them. Though they may actually mean well, they are not allowing you your process of discovery. The truth is that even if you do fail to reach your goals, your dreams and goals are *your* dreams and goals, and it is no one's right to discourage you from reaching them, even if they seem unrealistic or risky. Ultimately, you are the only one who can determine whether your goals are right for you.

If you are acting as the naysayer in your own life, ask yourself why you are allowing your inner critic to have so much power over your choices and actions. It may be that you have a bad habit of negative self-talk, or an overly self-critical nature, in which case, learning how to quiet that inner critic or change the narrative is imperative for your growth and well-being. This can be accomplished in many different ways, from working with a coach or therapist, to learning to meditate and replace the negative inner critic with the affirmative inner champion. It may be helpful for you to learn to write affirmations and say them out loud to yourself, or learn a technique to reprogram your thoughts. It is for you to determine whether your inner critic is keeping you from pursuing your dreams or is giving you some kind of guidance. However, if you're focused on the naysaying, you're not focused on your goal.

If you already have your road map figured out, and know what your actions need to be, then you already know what your possible obstacles are going to be. At that point, naysayers are not necessarily an obstacle; they are just people trying to deter you from your path, and whatever they have to say has no validity whatsoever. Naysayers should not have any authority in your life. They simply have an opinion that is not backed by anything real. They do not know what is in your heart or what you're capable of. Only you know that. I'm going to say it again: a naysayer is not an obstacle in your journey. Whether this person is your mother or best friend or you, the discouraging advice this person (or you yourself) is dispensing must be ignored if you are to reach your goals.

Defending yourself or arguing with a naysayer will only exhaust you and is one of the fastest ways to lose steam when developing or moving toward your goal. Listening to the naysayer is ultimately self-sabotaging; it is up to you to shut down the negative energy that is coming between you and your goal.

> *"Whatever you do. you need courage.*
>
> *Whatever course you decide upon,*
>
> *there is always someone to tell you that you are wrong."*
>
> *~ Ralph Waldo Emerson ~*

## The Gift of the Naysayer

I realize it's easy to *say* you must ignore the naysayer in your life, or in the case of your inner critic's voice, transform it or even vanquish it. However, it's an entirely different thing to actually have to *do* it. So, how does one go about moving past the naysayer, who, let's face it, is probably mirroring your own unspoken or sublimated self-doubt?

Naysayers are easy to recognize, even the passive-aggressive, "well-meaning" naysayers, because if they don't make you feel diminished in some way, they will irritate you or even piss you off. Their outright criticism or veiled "concern" will trigger your unspoken or unacknowledged self-doubt. This is actually a gift. They help you see where your vulnerabilities are and inspire you to be your own most fervent champion, your own most enthusiastic cheerleader. They move you to stand up for yourself and your dreams. They can even help you define your goals if you are not sure exactly what they are. Anger can be very activating, very motivating. In fact, an encounter with a naysayer may be the very thing to wake you up and activate your inner **Spirit**, your inner drive. It may be the aha! moment that turns everything around for you.

However, after recognizing the gift the naysayer has unwittingly bestowed, you will want to trade in your naysayer "friends" for a **Network** of true supporters. You may discover, when confronted by a naysayer, that you have to find a way to **Accept** your current situation and discover ways to **Cope** with the transition you're in before you have the bandwidth to define your goals. You will have to take full **Responsibility** for your choices, thoughts, actions, attitudes, and behaviors, past, present, and future, and **Risk** asking for help in defining and reaching your goals. And finally, you will want to define your **Goals** and the **Action** steps you will have to take to get where you want to go.

The principles laid out in this book—the Dedicated 8—are the tools you will need to employ in order to transform or vanquish both the inner and outer naysayers. In fact, if you simply follow the path outlined in this book, you may never feel the need to defend or explain yourself or your actions to anyone. By focusing on moving forward, by believing in yourself (even if you don't know exactly what you want to do), you will automatically shed the naysayers or convert them. Your own inner critic will quiet down as you follow this program and eventually transform into your inner guidance.

So, after you've gotten over the discouragement, shock, or anger that arises in the presence of a naysayer, remember to thank him or her (you can do this internally rather than expressing it to the person) for motivating you to stay your course, believe in and champion yourself, and train your focus on your dreams.

---

*"Keep away from people who try to belittle your ambitions. Small people always do that, but the really great make you feel that you, too, can become great.*
*When you are seeking to bring big plans to fruition, it is important with whom you regularly associate.*
*Hang out with friends who are like-minded and who are also designing purpose-filled lives.*
*Similarly, be that kind of a friend for your friends."*
*~ Mark Twain ~*

# Chapter Three

# Spirit

*"Gratitude bestows reverence, allowing us to encounter everyday epiphanies, those transcendent moments of awe that change forever how we experience life and the world."*

*~ John Milton ~*

**Choosing Love and Forgiveness**

In 2007, at the age of 27, 13 years into my sentence, a prison counselor asked me to come into his office. He handed me the telephone and said, "Your aunt is on the phone."

I said, "Who?"

He said, "Your Aunt Nancy."

I don't have an Aunt Nancy, but I said, "Hello."

When I heard her say hello, I realized who it was and I knew something was really wrong. It was my mom's best friend. She told me my mom was in the hospital dying of cancer, and the doctors didn't think she would live another 24 hours.

For $700 the prison would let me go see her on her deathbed for exactly one hour. Money in prison is very different from what it is in society. Inside prison, $50 is enough to buy you food for a whole month. So, coming up with $700 quickly was not an easy thing to do. However, I was able to make it happen because, even though I was starting to change my attitude and direct my energy toward creating a future for myself post release, I was hustling. I'd managed to get a cell phone and had a part in the flow of contraband into the prison. Drugs, tobacco, you name it, I could get it for you.

It would be the first time in 13 years that I would see my mother. It would also be the very last time I'd ever see her. I had a decision to make. I would have one hour with her, and it would be for the last time. I thought, *What do I do? Do I hold her accountable for everything? How do I let everything go, forgive her, and give her the best hour?*

I was driven to the hospital to see her. That car ride was a trip down memory lane. It had been 13 long years since I'd been in a car, and we drove past all the cities I'd lived in while in the foster care system and while living with my own parents. All I could think about was how the last hour with my mom would go.

As we traveled across the Tacoma Narrows Bridge, I looked out the windows, out at the sun reflecting off the water, and felt deeply peaceful. I knew in that moment that I wasn't going to hold anything against my mother. I would give her the best hour I could. I would tell her that she was a good mother and that I loved her very much. I thought about the fact that she'd had a tough life. She'd also been beaten by my stepdad. She was adopted. She'd had a rough childhood and had experienced a lot of the same challenges I had. So I chose in that moment, on that bridge, to let go, to forgive her and give her the best hour I could.

When I got to the hospital, I sat beside my mom and we looked over pictures and reminisced. I held her hand and told her I loved her. I knew this was the last time I would see her, touch her, tell her I loved her, or just be in her presence. The feeling I had leaving there was bittersweet; I was sad knowing I wouldn't see her again, but I also felt such a profound feeling of peace and freedom within, a feeling I hadn't had in a long time. I thought, *How can I take this feeling back?*

My inner smartass shot back, *Well, genius, how about you get rid of the cell phone and stop hustling when you get back to the prison?* I had seven years left in my sentence, and I decided I would spend these years doing things differently than I had up to this point. I gave up the hustle and started studying in earnest to prepare for my release.

> *"And the day came when the risk to remain tight in*
>
> *a bud was more painful*
>
> *than the risk it took to blossom." ~ Anaïs Nin ~*

## Awakening to Spirit

There is always some moment of epiphany, of profound realization, an aha! moment, or the moment when your spirit wakes up, before the awareness that your situation needs to change truly hits you. A person can experience many of these moments throughout a transformational process, and these moments can come at any time. Even though you can't force them, aha! moments don't happen in a vacuum. They don't "just happen"; they stem from your openness to these experiences, from your deep desire for answers to your questions, from your deep thought or prayer to solve the problems that confront you. In that sense they are self-generated. You just don't know when they're going to come to you.

When Oprah interviewed the author Eckhart Tolle about the meaning of the aha! moment, he explained it as a moment of true clarity. It is an awakening to the truth of your situation and clarity about what you want, or don't want, and the simultaneous awareness that you are willing to change your mindset in order to do something different, in order to create something different for yourself. For me, it's that moment when your spirit wakes up.

It's an internal awakening, a moment when you see the light. It's a moment that in an instant radically shifts your perception and position. It's the moment when the answer to your question or problem presents itself with clarity. It can be the answer to a creative problem or a solution to a personal problem. It can be inspiration or realization or resolution. It is a reckoning, the moment you *know* the answer. It can come to you in a moment of extreme discomfort or grief, and it can come to you in a moment of profound creative inquiry or elation.

> *"When we are no longer able to change a situation,*
>
> *we are challenged to change ourselves."*
>
> *~ Viktor E. Frankl ~*

## The Green Beanie

To understand the following story it is important to know that prison is completely racially segregated. If you're a fan of the TV show, *Orange Is the New Black,* imagine that. Everything is racially segregated in prison, from who you live with and where you eat to where you exercise, what showers you use, and who you sit with in your classes. Whites with whites, blacks with blacks, Asians with Asians, etc. That's just the way it is. I got along with a lot of different people in prison, so I had friends of all races, but our day-to-day living as dictated by the prison system required racial separation.

A white friend of mine had a disagreement with an Asian friend of mine. He went to my Asian friend's place of work, beat him pretty badly, and got out before he got caught. The Asian guy was so messed up that he looked like he had "elephant man" disease when they took him to medical. I think the reason for the beating was that the Asian guy had disrespected my friend by calling him a "rat." Being a rat or a sex offender in prison is the worst of the worst.

Later in the day the guards came and took my white friend to segregation, or solitary confinement. Segregation is also referred to as "the hole" or "the box" and sometimes "the SHU" (special housing units). Rumor had it that a black guy in the unit they lived in told on him. He was developmentally disabled in some way. He probably told, but he also probably didn't know any better. However, my white friend was pretty popular, so the white population decided they were going to take care of the black guy. A white guy went into the black guy's cell and did a lot of damage to him. When the black guys saw that this guy was beaten up as badly as he was, they assumed that two people had jumped him.

So as soon as lockdown was over, two black guys decided to jump a white guy, and then two white guys jumped a black guy. That happened several times until the prison decided to lock everybody down so they could figure out what the hell was going on. What they didn't understand was that lockdown actually fueled the fire because tensions were being built up behind locked doors and eventually when they opened those doors, it was going to happen again and on a bigger scale. Rumors started to spread between the inmates that when we came off lockdown, we were all going to head to the gym. We were not going to do any more of these two-on-one fights. We were going to just get it all out of the way and get down with everybody.

Everybody was saying, "Get prepared." We were going to get into a major brawl where anyone could get stabbed. So, "come with a weapon" was what they were saying. Be prepared. We got off lockdown and, sure enough, everybody started filing into the gym—whites with whites, blacks with blacks, Hispanics with Hispanics, Natives with Natives, and Asians with Asians. As we walked in, we were all very alert. The whites lined up against one wall, the blacks lined up against another, and so on. This never happened, so the guards were freaking out while we all lined up against the walls.

Guys had brought shanks, makeshift knives, with them. One of them was a friend of mine who happened to be standing next to me. He'd created the shank out of a busted coat hanger and a razor. He'd brought a few of them and gave me one. Everybody was ready to defend himself. We all had shanks—all of us. I looked across the gym and saw some black guys who were my friends and some Natives who were friends, and I thought, *This is a nightmare.* I was scared. I was watching one white guy pacing back and forth yelling, "Fuck these motherfuckers, fuck these n####rs, fuck them... Let's fucking do this." I was thinking, *You're going to get us killed, bro. You are such an idiot. You're about to put all our lives in danger.*

Finally, the sergeant, who was a woman, came out to the middle of the gym with a fire extinguisher. She started bellowing, "Listen to me right now. I'm not fucking doing this. I don't care what your problems are. I don't care what you're going through, but this is not the answer to any of this. You don't even know the people that were in any of the fights. It ain't happening in my gym. It's not happening today and you're not fighting here and if you do, I'm going to spray you right in the face with this fire extinguisher."

She was not joking. You could tell how serious she was. She yelled, "You guys are going back to the unit. I'm following you out. Race by race. And if anyone makes a move, you're going right into the hole."

We were talking among ourselves trying to decide whether we were going to listen to her. The majority of guys were saying, "Let's watch the blacks, because the blacks have to go first. And if they just walk out without doing anything, we'll call it good."

The black guys would usually make you think they were going to leave, then attack you when you let your guard down. So we waited for that. In the end they walked out without making a move. We knew we would be the third group out, and while we were waiting, I looked down the line and saw a green beanie coming toward me from man to man. When you go to prison you are supplied with "state-issue clothing," which generally includes a brown beanie. This one just happened to be green. By the time I got it, it was packed full of so many weapons I thought it might rip apart. Frankly, I was impressed with the ingenuity of some of the weapons. As I put my shank in that hat, I realized I was lucky to be alive and leaving that gym. I knew full well that my life could have ended that day.

As I walked out, I looked over at the pull-up bar next to the guard's desk and saw the green beanie full of all the shanks just sitting on the floor near that bar. It would eventually be found by the guards, of course, but for the moment the guards couldn't see it. When I saw it sitting there, bursting with weapons, I again felt so grateful to be alive.

By the time I got back to the unit, my mindset had changed. I knew I wanted something better for myself. This was truly a moment of clarity. I knew very well I could have lost my life in that place, and realized I needed to reset my way of thinking and living so I would never be in that situation again. So what was I going to do? It would be a few years before I figured out what I wanted, but that's the moment everything changed for me, and I started thinking about my future.

## What's in It for Me?

The message of this chapter is be open to those unplanned, unexpected moments in life that have the power to completely reverse your course, change your mindset, put you on the right track, open you up to new opportunities, expand your horizons, offer creative solutions, and put you in touch with something greater than yourself. If you believe that human beings have free will, what does that mean to you? Do we have complete "control" over the course of our lives? I would say no. But we do have the opportunity to choose, in every moment, to respond in one way or another to everything that crosses our path. The free will to choose our attitude.

Will you choose to open your heart and mind to love and forgiveness, to life? Or will you choose to live with hatred, regret, and vengeance in your heart and soul? The choice is yours. You will be faced with moments throughout your life that will ask you to choose one path or the other. I encourage you to choose life and love, forgiveness and gratitude, kindness and generosity, happiness and wonder, curiosity and attention.

Choose yourself. Be present for yourself and create within yourself the experience you want to have in the world, with others, in relationships, and at work. In other words, cultivate self-love, self-acceptance, self-appreciation, self-esteem, and self-respect so that when Spirit gives you an undeniable choice to move forward toward love and opportunity, you will have the courage to risk opening your heart and soul. You ultimately have the choice to embrace or deny life. There are no guarantees of a particular kind of "success" in life, and your dreams, more often than not, come to you in a form you hadn't anticipated, *but* if you act out of love, more times than not you will receive love in return.

> *"A single event can awaken within us a stranger totally unknown to us. To live is to be slowly born."*
>
> *~ Antoine de Saint-Exupéry ~*

## Exercises

At the end of each chapter I've included exercises to help you put the Dedicated 8 into practice. Here are the exercises for this chapter, which could help to create a space in which an aha! moment can occur:

1.  Think back over your life and identify and list some of the aha! moments you've had—those moments when you've experienced a sudden insight or intuition about something, when some aspect of your life became clear and it had a profound effect on you. (You may be surprised how many you've had.) It could even have been a significant emotional release.

2.  Choose a few of the more significant, life-changing moments, and try to remember what led up to them. Was it deep thinking about a particular problem? Was it holding a question in your mind for weeks on end? Was it deep prayer or meditation? Did it happen when you were relaxed and not thinking about anything in particular?

3. If you find yourself needing answers or solutions to nagging questions or problems, try to duplicate what you did, perhaps unwittingly, in the past that created those moments. You can't force these aha! moments when Spirit touches you, but you *can* be open and set the stage for them to occur.

# Chapter Four

# Acceptance

*"Accept—then act. Whatever the present moment contains,*

*accept it as if you had chosen it....*

*This will miraculously transform your whole life."*

~ Eckhart Tolle ~

**Breaking Up Is Hard to Do**

Just before I started writing this book, my life changed dramatically. On Martin Luther King Jr. Day 2018, my girlfriend of two years broke up with me. My feelings are still raw, and I've been working through my hurt and anger in an effort to get to a place of **Acceptance**. I believe I am finally there, and I want to share with you a little of what I experienced and how I worked my process to get to acceptance.

I wanted to marry her. The truth is I still want to marry her even after all the pain and ugliness of our breakup. I've been on the other side. I've been the person who did the breaking up. Looking back, they were difficult moments, but it was actually relatively easy for me to work through my feelings on that side of it. Being on this side has been very difficult and painful. In fact, it wasn't until this morning as I write this that acceptance finally aligned with my mind and came into my body and heart.

My mind had previously "accepted" that we were broken up. I'd mentally acknowledged that I probably wouldn't see her again, that she's going to have another guy in her life, and that she's going to move on without me. In my mind I could see her fading away, just like in the movies when a character who has been affected by a change in the past is staring at a photo and the person in the photo starts to disappear. In my mind I've seen her disappearing from many different pictures of our lives together. But until this morning, I was still yearning for her in my heart. I was still longing and pining and hoping that somehow I would at the very least hear from her.

It has been quite intense. Since we broke up, my life has turned upside down. I moved out of her house and reached out to friends for a place to live while I was regrouping because I wasn't financially able to rent anywhere at the moment. None of my friends in the Seattle area had a long-term place for me, so some good friends in Las Vegas offered to let me stay in their RV. I drove down to Las Vegas contemplating the entire time what it would take for me to start over in a different city, in a different state. Could I just start over from zero in a place I'd never lived in?

When I got there I was emotionally distraught. I hadn't started using any tools of acceptance to get over the breakup. Adding to my overwhelming emotions, this RV triggered my memories of growing up in a trailer and my feelings of being a failure. Sitting in that trailer, looking at all my stuff, which barely fit, was just too much. I needed to get away from there. I needed to be able to clear my mind. I needed to find somewhere I could heal—away from people, away from things that would make me depressed, away from my everyday life.

I'd recently had an opportunity to take a trip to Jakarta, Indonesia, and had felt at peace there. So I decided then and there to get on a plane and go back to Jakarta, which is where I am right this minute, recording my thoughts about this journey I've been on. As soon as I arrived in Jakarta, I knew I had to come to the place where I'd be able to start my journey toward acceptance.

I've been here in Jakarta for a few weeks, and every day I've felt sadness. I've felt frustration. I've felt heartache. I've wondered why this is happening to me and I've asked God, "Why? Why me? What's next? What's my journey?" I've been waking up every day without communicating with my ex-girlfriend. Waking up every day without her next to me. Waking up every day knowing that our goals and dreams are not going to happen. Waking up every day knowing that there might be somebody else in her life. Waking up every day knowing there's going to be somebody else in my life eventually. Waking up every day knowing that the things we used to like to do together are not going to happen again.

My process—the intense self-inquiry, prayer, meditation, and release of emotions—has finally allowed me to accept all those truths. One of the things I found myself doing as a way to symbolically cleanse my feelings and thoughts was to meditate in the shower. I turned on the shower and lay down in the bathtub, allowing the water to pour over my body as I closed my eyes and quieted my mind. I've also gone on long, meditative, meandering walks. And believe it or not, I've been researching about how to recover from heartbreak. This activity might seem more like a coping skill, which will be covered in the next chapter, but because it is still part of the inner process of healing and coming to a place of acceptance, I consider it to be a useful tool for moving toward acceptance.

I wanted to understand my situation. I've never experienced heartache like this. I started reading article after article, and in the end they all basically said the same thing: forgive, look at yourself, stay active, keep your mind straight, move on. All these things combined—the walking and exercising, researching, meditating—led me to being able to finally accept the situation. My mind and body have come together, and I feel at peace and at one with acceptance. (A few times in this book I refer to your mind and body coming together. What I mean by this I mean that you not only feel it and understand whatever the situation is in your mind, but you *feel* it in your body. For example, have you ever been upset about something or at someone and your mind lets you say that you forgive them but you really don't feel it in your body yet? That is because your mind and body have not come together in how it feels about the situation or person. That coming together feeling is what I am referring to.

You might be asking yourself, "This guy has been through so much hard stuff in his life, why is he so messed up over a relationship?" The truth is, this was a totally new, emotionally charged experience for me, completely unlike anything I'd ever experienced. I haven't had the chance to be in relationships and go through breakups the way most people have. I went to prison at 14 years old and got out when I was 31. I use this recent example from my own life to relay to you that even at this stage in my evolution, despite having overcome the struggles of my earlier life, and despite having succeeded at the career of my dreams, I must still use the Dedicated 8 to move forward. And I expect to continue applying these principals as I deal with the changing circumstances that come up throughout my life.

> *Acceptance of what has happened is the first step*
>
> *to overcoming the consequences of any misfortune.*
>
> *~ William James ~*

## Accepting the Unacceptable

Acceptance is the full realization of and surrender to your present situation, whether you like it or not. Generally speaking, it is easy to accept a situation you like. In fact, you probably don't even think about whether you can or will "accept" it, because it's not challenging you, it's not forcing you to think about how you'd really like to be in a different situation. Ironically, the situation you do not like is the one I'm encouraging you to accept. This doesn't mean I'm encouraging you to capitulate, submit, or give up. I'm encouraging you to surrender (in the sense that you cease resistance), to be in the reality of your current situation, to take stock, to face it and yourself.

Without acceptance there can be no forward movement. If you are fighting with yourself and your situation, if you are in denial about where you are or what's happening, you are not present. When you are not present, you cannot accurately assess your situation and you cannot make self-honoring decisions. If you are not in acceptance, you are in reaction. What does that mean? When you react, you are acting against it, you are not in control, and you are allowing your circumstances to manipulate you. When you accept, you are able to respond rather than react. When you respond to a situation, it means you have a measure of control over your choices, and you're able to rationally consider various options and make healthier, more self-supporting choices.

Acceptance is both a state of being and a mindset that comes through awareness and intention. I see where I am. I may not like it, but it is my current reality. My intention is to accept the current reality of my situation and take full responsibility for this moment so I can evaluate how I got here and begin to formulate a plan for creating a different and more desirable reality.

You can recognize your own resistance to acceptance if you catch yourself blaming another person, or blaming the circumstance you think got you into the situation you're currently in. Interestingly, resistance can be enabled in the form of "support." Your friends may want to keep talking negatively about your situation. They may be keeping the blame spiral going without realizing that they are not actually supporting you but are in fact disempowering you. It is up to you to recognize and move away from the outside influences that are keeping you in resistance.

Trying to move forward without accepting your current situation first is like building a house without a foundation. Acceptance is the foundation. You can't move on when you're in a state of denial or a state of fantasy or when you're living in the past or the future. Though you generally find yourself having to accept an outer situation or circumstance, acceptance is an inner state of being, the moment when you fully connect with yourself. It's the moment when you confront and get honest with yourself about who you are and why you are in the situation you're in. Acceptance is about owning your situation, whether you like it or not. You don't have to like it to accept it.

> *"Accept what comes to you totally and completely so that you can appreciate it, learn from it, and then let it go."*
>
> *~ Deepak Chopra ~*

## Jessica Vanlandingham's Story

Jessica is a good friend who has an important lesson to share about how she learned to accept her situation while she strategized different ways to move forward toward her goals. Here is her story, in her own words:

I had a really rough childhood, and I've dealt with every kind of abuse you could imagine. I'm thirty-seven now and have four kids. The oldest is eighteen and the youngest is three. I had just turned nineteen when I had my first child, and because I wanted to be a good mom, I started working at a bank. Then I had my second child, my son. Sadly, during the course of my four-year relationship with his father, I endured domestic violence and started using drugs again. I'd struggled with addiction since I was 13. The first time I went to rehab I was 17, and at 22 I fell off the wagon for a while and ended up going to jail several times. With the encouragement of someone I met in jail, I opted for drug court, which I did for three years.

A few years later I started working in the corporate offices of T-Mobile. I loved the job, but within a year of starting I went through a divorce with the father of my third child and ended up getting fired. I was just not able to concentrate on the job. During that time I also got evicted from my home and was in an extremely bad car accident that almost killed me and three other people. At that point I went back to drugs.

In 2014 I got pulled over in a stolen vehicle and went back to jail. When I got out, I decided it was time to clean up my life for good, and through a series of serendipitous circumstances ended up in a sales position for a marketing and website development company run by an old friend from childhood. Even though I was lucky to get that job, being in a job because you feel like there is no other option can be disheartening.

I was feeling called to volunteer for the Prison Ministries after all I'd been through, but my determination to find a way to support myself and get my children back meant I had to find a position that paid well. Right now this job is paying my bills and enabling me to support my family. And though I'm good at my job, it feels somewhat hollow. I'm not living my dream, but I have to stay in this position until I can figure out how to create a different opportunity, one that will be fulfilling and lucrative.

I've been able to accept my situation because I'm so deeply grateful for the financial stability it has given me. I accept that my first priority is to my family; nonetheless, I think about how to move toward my dreams and goals all the time. I pray a lot, I pray at work, I pray all the time. This includes a lot of positive self-talk. I encourage myself by telling myself that I'm doing a good job and that I will eventually reach my goals. I write inspirational notes to myself. Sometimes it's something I've heard somebody say, or something I've thought of, or a realization I've had. I write these things down on Post-it notes and stick them in front of me wherever I am.

I also spend a lot of time teaching myself different skills. These are things I've been interested in or think I might like to do at some point in my life. I've taught myself graphic design and how to build websites. I've studied marketing and interior design. I do a lot of different things just to keep myself busy, but I'm also always exploring my options by trying new things.

***

The gratitude Jessica feels for the financial stability she's gained from staying in a job that isn't her dream is a powerful attitude to cultivate in any process of moving toward acceptance—supported by prayer, positive self-talk, and writing down affirmations and inspirational messages. This doesn't mean I'm necessarily encouraging you to stay in a job or position you don't like, but from a mindset of acceptance you are far more likely to make self-honoring choices.

Jessica also demonstrates a creative approach to finding acceptance by opening her mind to opportunities to learn new skills and information. The next chapter focuses on coping as a strategy for healing and moving forward. I must note here that some of the steps Jessica makes to keep herself occupied, stimulated, and inspired (taking classes and doing research) are more aligned with my definition of coping than they are with strategies for moving into acceptance. However, there are no hard lines here. As you move toward acceptance, you may find yourself alternating between working your inner process while exploring outer opportunities for growth and expansion. You may even find, as did Jessica, that while you are working toward acceptance, you are also beginning to take action toward goals—all of which will be covered in later chapters.

This attests to the fact that the process of changing your mindset and transforming your life is a holistic process that will ask you to employ many different tools and strategies in different ways and at different times as you support yourself physically, mentally, emotionally, and spiritually in your journey toward the realization of your goals.

> *"To complain is always nonacceptance of what is. It*
>
> *invariably carries an unconscious negative charge.*
>
> *When you complain, you make yourself a victim.*
>
> *Leave the situation or accept it. All else is madness."*
>
> *~ Eckhart Tolle ~*

## Useful Tools

The tools that can get you to a place of acceptance are those used in many disciplines and practices that encourage an inner process of self-healing and transformation. First and foremost, I encourage you to express your emotions—cry, scream into a pillow, punch a pillow, exercise, dance, or engage in free-form writing to release anger and sadness (then burn the pages without rereading them). Each time you release your emotions, I encourage you to practice any of the following tools that appeal to you: meditate, pray, create affirmations and say them out loud, engage in positive self-talk, research your situation, walk in nature, do yoga, rest, engage in self-care, and commit random acts of kindness. If these tools are not familiar to you, I encourage you to seek out support from institutions, teachers, therapists, and coaches who teach various forms of inner work. You might check out your local Zen center, yoga studio, church, synagogue, spiritual center, or botanical garden.

For those of you who are going through a particularly tough time in your life and are finding it impossible to move into a place of acceptance, please know that you are not alone. There is no time limit on this process. However, if you're harming or wanting to harm yourself or others, my recommendation is that you seek help immediately in the form of a therapist, spiritual counselor, coach, or doctor.

> *"Right now, despite your education level, despite your family history, despite your level of intelligence, despite anything, you have the power to reach your wealth goals. As soon as you believe that, you are ready to accept what you deserve."*
>
> *~ David Osborn and Paul Morris,* Wealth Can't Wait *~*

## Acceptance as a Practice

Acceptance is not necessarily easy, but it is absolutely necessary. That's why it comes first after Spirit.

An encounter with Spirit or an encounter that wakes your spirit cannot be predicted or planned and may come at the beginning, middle, or end of a transformational journey, but acceptance must come before any of the other principles can be effectively practiced or applied.

Without acceptance you are in resistance, and that state of being will impact everything you do or attempt to do. Resistance will make everything harder and may become so intractable that you just give up. You may become so exhausted, depressed, disillusioned, or disheartened that you stop truly living on some level. The only answer to resistance, to refusal, is acceptance. Again, I repeat: You do not have to like your situation, but you must accept it before you can change it to your benefit or move on from it.

As with an encounter with Spirit, when faced with the challenge to accept a situation you do not like or want, you have a choice. But it may not feel like you have a choice. Your emotions may lead you to believe it is impossible for you to accept your situation, but that is simply not true. Remember, I know what I'm talking about. Seventeen years in prison makes me an expert. It took some time, years even, but I ultimately accepted a situation I did not want. That is the reason I am free and prospering today.

If I had resisted my situation, I might have been so filled with increasing resentment and anger that I'd be dead today, or back in prison. I might have become an addict, or been released with absolutely no skills to survive in the outside world. But because I accepted my life as it was, I was able to explore opportunities and open my mind and heart to assistance, education, relationships, and resources.

There is a reason some people consider acceptance to be a spiritual practice. It often entails the invocation of a higher power, or manifesting a higher aspect of yourself. When your emotions or long-held beliefs tell you that you can't, your higher self (or the divinity within) will tell you that you can. By forgiving yourself first and then all others you feel have wronged you, and all the political or social institutions that have let you down or never supported you in the first place, you can begin to see your way out of your situation with greater clarity.

Life is not fair. Some people will always get more, have access to more, or be given more. Some people are lucky, charmed, or have "good karma." Some people are born with movie star looks, genius, talent, great health, and sanity. But none of this really matters. What matters is *you*. You are unique, and in your uniqueness you are beautiful and worthy. You were born for a reason, and it is your mission to discover what it is and how to fulfil it. As Rick Warren says in *The Purpose Driven Life,* "You were made for a mission.... Fulfilling your mission in the world is God's purpose for your life." If you are always in resistance, or comparing yourself to others you deem more fortunate, or just resenting your situation, you will never discover your unique purpose on the planet.

Of course we all want to live well, be healthy and fulfilled, but regardless of your circumstances, you can always find a way to improve your situation. However, you must first find peace and calm within. Decisions or actions made from a mindset of fear, desperation, or fury will never get you the level of success or freedom that decisions made from the mindset of acceptance or peace within will. As Dr. Daniel Amen writes in *Change Your Brain, Change Your Life,* "When your brain works right, you work right. But when your brain is troubled, you are much more likely to have trouble in your life. With a healthy brain, you are happier, physically healthier (because you make better decisions), wealthier (also because you make better decisions) and more successful in everything you do. When your brain is unhealthy, for whatever reason, you are sadder, sicker, poorer and less successful."

Make getting to a place of acceptance a practice, especially if you are feeling challenged by your circumstances. Use the various tools I have recommended, do the exercises at the end of this chapter, and you will eventually, perhaps sooner than you think, find yourself relaxing and breathing more easily. You will gain clarity and a feeling of inner strength that will positively inform your next move. From that place you are much more likely to end up in a situation that is supportive, that will feed you and give you the tools to move toward your ultimate goals in life.

"*Ultimately, acceptance is about trusting yourself to rise to whatever occasion presents itself to you.*

*It is about being open to ALL of life, knowing that it all has value whether you like it or not.*"

*~ Judith Johnson ~*

## Exercises

Now it's your turn. Here are some questions and exercises to help you move into acceptance:

1. Write down a few situations you've had trouble accepting.

2. Did you ultimately accept them? If you did, how did you do it?

3. If you didn't, do you think you could by using the tools recommended in this chapter? Which tools resonate with you most, and which do you think you would be willing to try?

4. Think of a situation you are experiencing now that you're having trouble accepting. This could be something like a breakup, losing your job, a decision you have to make, waiting for someone to call you back, or some other thing you need to internally accept before moving forward. Apply the practices and tools that resonate with you and see if you can change your mindset.

5. If you wish to take this exercise to the next level, keep a daily diary of your process and progress. You don't have to write a memoir, just jot notes about what works, what doesn't, and what you've noticed in your own inner world. Do you feel more accepting when you meditate, or do you feel better after a walk? Does being with people help, or does it make you feel worse? Keep experimenting until you find a few different exercises that help you get to and maintain a feeling of equanimity, inner peace, or acceptance.

**Remember:** The **F** in **FREEDOM** is for **Focusing** on your present circumstance and feeling your **Feelings.**

# Chapter Five

# Coping

*"Life is not what it's supposed to be. It's what it is.*

*The way you cope with it is what makes the difference."*

*~ Virginia Satir ~*

**Doing Time Playing Chess**

In March 1995, the prison inmates decided they were going to protest the fact that the prison took 35 percent of the money their family members sent them. They planned to protest by refusing to go to work, refusing to cook the meals, and refusing to go to school. I was fifteen at the time, just one year too young to work in the State of Washington, so I was unable to take part in the work stoppage.

My "program" (a term used by the prison system to refer to what you do during the day—a work program or a school program) was going to school. When the inmates who were supposed to cook breakfast refused to work, the entire prison was locked down at 4:00 a.m. Because I was in "closed custody," I was not allowed to go to school that morning. However, the "medium custody" inmates, who had more freedom than I did, were not subject to the lockdown and were allowed to go to work and to school.

A couple of days on lockdown went by and the guards, who had dressed up in riot gear (we called them the "goon squad" when they were in riot gear), came to get me to take me to segregation. In the movies, segregation is referred to as "the hole" or "the box" and sometimes "the SHU" (Special Housing Units). It is exactly what the word indicates. You are segregated from everyone and everything. You are in a cell 23 and sometimes 24 hours a day. It's a cold and lonely place, one that that forces you to think, reflect, mourn, dream, exercise, cry, and persevere.

They said I'd participated in an organized work stoppage and had threatened the medium-custody inmates. As I explained above, I had not participated in the work stoppage because again, I was too young to be allowed to work, and I had not said anything to the medium-custody prisoners. I've never known why they picked me up that day. However, it had an impact on my life for the next year.

At my hearing in segregation, when I was asked how I would plead, I said, "All the guards are laughing at this infraction because I wasn't able to participate in anything. I wasn't able to do what I'm being charged with. We were already on lockdown long before I was supposed to go to my class." The hearing officer wrote that my statement was "I laugh at this infraction." They gave me a year straight in segregation. A year, at 15 years old, for supposedly participating in a work strike when I didn't even have a job.

At 15 years old I had to reset my mindset to survive that year in solitary confinement without going crazy. And the very first thing I had to do was accept my situation. I had to accept that I was not going to come out of that room for 23 hours a day and that there was nothing I could do about it. So, how did I **cope** with being in segregation? How did I keep myself from going crazy or becoming desperately depressed?

I read books, I drew, I wrote poetry. I got a radio at one point, so I listened to music. I exercised. I wrote letters. And... I played chess with the other inmates. We made a chessboard with numbers and played chess for hours upon hours upon hours upon hours. To make chess boards, we each drew 64 squares on a sheet of paper (as you can see on the next page). The chess pieces were torn bits of toilet paper marked to indicate what they were: "P" for pawn, "R" for rook, etc. Then we would yell out our moves to each other: "49 to 33..." You get the idea.

| 1 | 2 | 3 | 4 | 5 | 6 | 7 | 8 |
|---|---|---|---|---|---|---|---|
| 9 | 10 | 11 | 12 | 13 | 14 | 15 | 16 |
| 17 | 18 | 19 | 20 | 21 | 22 | 23 | 24 |
| 25 | 26 | 27 | 28 | 29 | 30 | 31 | 32 |
| 33 | 34 | 35 | 36 | 37 | 38 | 39 | 40 |
| 41 | 42 | 43 | 44 | 45 | 46 | 47 | 48 |
| 49 | 50 | 51 | 52 | 53 | 54 | 55 | 56 |
| 57 | 58 | 59 | 60 | 61 | 62 | 63 | 64 |

Interestingly, learning to cope with my situation brought out my natural curiosity and creativity and made me more disciplined and resourceful. I learned not only to survive but thrive to the best of my ability under the circumstances.

> *"I choose not to think of my life as surviving, but coping."*
>
> *~ Lorna Luft ~*

## Coping Strategies

**Coping** is both an extension of what you are doing as you move toward greater acceptance of your situation, and the next step in transforming your life. It is a shift from the *inner* focus of acceptance to an *outer* focus of dealing with your circumstances, which serves to relieve stress as well as reset your perspective. You are not necessarily taking **action steps** toward your **goals** yet, you are simply dealing with the stress of your situation in healthy ways. Coping also gives you the opportunity to change your entrenched negative patterns by doing different things or doing things differently than you've done in the past.

Following is a list of suggestions of things you can choose to do to help you cope with your situation: exercising, writing poetry, journaling about what you're feeling, seeing a movie, singing, punching a punching bag, taking a nap, being with your pet, going shopping, cleaning, reading, listening to music, meditating, going out in nature, painting, shooting hoops, writing letters or emails, going dancing, cooking, going for a drive, completing a task, reading spiritually uplifting books or any books for that matter, communicating with your friends, throwing a party, riding your bicycle, searching for ridiculous things on the internet, performing random acts of kindness, serving dinner at a soup kitchen, picking up trash along a nature trail, babysitting your niece, visiting your grandmother, planning a trip, traveling. The list goes on and on.

The point is, there are many, many things you can do with your time that may not be leading you directly toward your ultimate goal, but will keep you occupied, keep your focus off yourself, and give you a break from your pain. This is not to say that meditating or inward reflection are bad or undesirable, but there are times when your pain makes it challenging to stay positive and clear-headed. Yes, processing your feelings and self-reflection are certainly important and absolutely necessary to your recovery and general health, but there are moments after you've cried and meditated when you just need something simple to distract you from dwelling on what it is you don't like or why you are so unhappy.

The beauty of coping is that you can sometimes discover skills, interests, and activities that change your life and even become action steps toward your goal or give you some clarity about what you really want to do. Coping can lead you to new friends, help you get fit and healthy, and expose you to experiences you might never have had otherwise. So, don't worry about feeling like you don't have a direction...yet. Allow yourself time and space to play, fool around, tinker, experiment, meander, explore, goof off, heal, recover, grow, and express your creativity. You are worth it!

Your situation may not please you, but after you have accepted where you are for the time being, you can choose to make the best of it by putting your focus on activities that are uplifting, energizing, and healthy. You do not have to push yourself. The point is *not* to create more stress but to relieve stress so you can begin to think about your goals and dreams. It is extremely difficult to put your attention on what you really want if all you are focused on is what you don't want or don't like. That said, knowing what you don't want can be valuable because it can give you clarity and ultimately help you focus on where you'd prefer to be putting your attention.

In all this work it is important to be kind to yourself, to love yourself through your process, and to learn to be your own cheerleader. Cultivating coping skills is a great way to support your own development and appreciate yourself. The more you release stress and begin to find joy, the faster you will be able to change your situation. Move toward the life you want!

> "I'm proud of the way I've dealt with setbacks. It's hard
>
> when you feel down
>
> and you think, 'Why is the world doing this to me?'
>
> But you have to pick yourself up again.
>
> That's what makes you a better athlete."
>
> ~ Jessica Ennis ~

## My Coping Methods

This brings me back to how I coped with losing my relationship, now that I have been able to accept the loss. How do you cope with something so traumatizing, something that just destroyed your world? Well, I changed my environment drastically to give myself space from everything and everyone. I needed to take my mind off my life. Now that I'm here in Jakarta, Indonesia, coping for me has consisted of creating a plan for my day and sticking to it so my mind and time are occupied and I'm moving forward in a positive direction, rather than spiraling down into depression and despair. I'm exploring Jakarta. I'm appreciating new places and different customs. I've been walking every day and paying attention to all the different kinds of relationships I'm observing. I'm trying different foods and meeting new people.

I've also been staying in touch with friends back home who are selflessly supportive of me. My friend Christina has been amazing—messaging me every day, video calling, making sure I'm okay, just caring about me, which has been deeply healing and uplifting. I have also made a commitment to myself to breathe a few breaths of unstressed air every day. I stand outside and breathe in and breathe out without thinking about anything that upsets me. I also make sure I smile about something unrelated to anything going on in my life every day.

Another coping strategy I've come up with is finding someone locally whom I can honor or appreciate in a big way. The other night I went out to dinner and there were four or five of us eating at this restaurant. They stayed open late for us and all their staff stayed. They weren't trying to rush us, and they were very kind, so I gave a generous tip for the service and the food and for them being willing to wait around for us to finish. When we finally walked out, all of the staff stood up and thanked me individually for coming to the restaurant. They all gave a gracious bow and expressed their appreciation. It was very humbling and made me feel grateful to be alive!

## Hal Elrod's S.A.V.E.R.S.

While I was in Jakarta, after I began to accept my situation, I asked myself, "How do I continue to deal with and transform this pain?" One of the books that was most helpful to me was Hal Elrod's *The Miracle Morning*. He outlines a list of activities (Life S.A.V.E.R.S.) that make up and create the miracle morning. If you're not familiar with Hal's book, you should definitely check it out and practice his activities in your life. Hal's Life S.A.V.E.R.S. turned out to be a great coping strategy for me: **S** for **Silence**; **A** for **Affirmations**; **V** for **Visualization**; **E** for **Exercise**; **R** for **Reading**; and **S** for **Scribing**.

I practiced **silence** by meditating (in my room, or as described earlier, in my shower) and praying, both of which helped me to cope and also to keep moving toward full acceptance of my situation.

I love **affirmations**. Saying them out loud was an important part of my process and recovery. Some of my affirmations were:

I deserve a great life!

I deserve a strong, loving person in my life!

If I change nothing, then nothing will change!

I intend to live like no one else, so I can LIVE like no one else! (borrowed from Dave Ramsey)

I have the choice to change right now in this moment!

I am a good person who enjoys helping people. I am *amazing* at it!

I used **visualization** as a way to encourage myself to keep thinking about this book and what I wanted to express and how I wanted the whole process to unfold. This is a great tool for goal setting, and something to use in that process, but it is also useful as a coping tool when you need to get something done while you are trying to get through something difficult, challenging, or painful.

I spent every day **exercising**. I walked around the city of Jakarta and went swimming and running quite often, all of which helped to keep me sane and metaphorically moving forward toward recovery and my goals.

I was **reading** all the time, doing research for the book, as well as reading about how to deal with my breakup.

The **scribing** (journaling) I did was for release and self-expression, as well as for this book.

The Life S.A.V.E.R.S. not only helped me cope with my circumstances, but gave me a discipline and focus I would not have had otherwise. As I've written in this chapter, there are many great coping strategies and activities, but if you are looking for something structured and comprehensive, I can't recommend Hal Elrod's program enough.

> *"Resilience isn't a single skill. It's a variety of*
>
> *skills and coping mechanisms.*
>
> *To bounce back from bumps in the road as well as failures,*
>
> *you should focus on emphasizing the positive."*
>
> *~ Jean Chatzky ~*

## Exercises

Your turn:

1. Write down some of the coping strategies you've used in the past.

2. Did they help you feel better, less stressed? If they did, how did they help?

3. If they didn't, do you think the tools recommended in this chapter might help you? Which tools resonate with you the most?

4. Even if you're not currently in a situation that requires a coping strategy to weather it, would you be willing to explore some of the tools and strategies mentioned?

5. How do the coping strategies you picked make you feel? Relaxed, stimulated, relieved, energized? Keep exploring until you find a few different tools that make you feel uplifted or calm.

6. If you *are* struggling with a difficult situation, I advise the same approach. Keep experimenting until you find several different coping strategies that take your mind off your problems and give you some relief.

**Remember:** The **R** in **FREEDOM** stands for **Research, Rest** and **Recreation.**

# <u>Chapter Six</u>

# Responsibility

*"If you don't take responsibility for anything, you are a*

*tiny ball in the world's pinball machine. You get blasted*

*from one bumper to the next. None of it is in your control.*

*Conversely, if you choose to take responsibility for*

*everything -- your past, your present, and your future --*

*suddenly you are 100% in control."*

*~ David Osborn and Paul Morris,* Wealth Can't Wait *~*


**The Apology Letter**

In 2009, two years after my mother died, I wrote an apology letter to David, the man whose car I'd attempted to steal when I was 14. This was my second letter; the first was never delivered. In my letter I wrote, "I'm very sorry for my actions.... I write you this because it wasn't until after losing my mom and rereading your letter to the judge that I fully understood what effect my actions had on your whole life." I described how I was trying to better myself, that I'd read a lot of books and taken a lot of classes. I told him I was studying to be a real estate agent. I went on to write, "You asked where my conscience and morality were, as if I didn't have either at the time. At 14 years old with the upbringing I had, it wasn't that I lacked these two traits. I believe they weren't taught to me properly and that I didn't truly understand them yet. I just want to express that I'm truly sorry for my bad choices and actions that day."

I had to write that letter to David because I couldn't move forward until I'd expressed my remorse. It was eating at me and making me feel extremely uncomfortable. I knew that the only way I could relieve my discomfort and move on was to take full responsibility for what I'd done by apologizing to him, even if he never accepted my apology. I wrote the letter because I genuinely felt sorry for what I'd done and wanted him to know that, but I also wrote the letter for my own peace of mind. It was a way for me to start forgiving myself.

To move toward any goal, you have to have a clear mind. You have to have a clear perspective. If there's anything in the way, keeping you from moving forward—your thoughts, feelings, judgments, or regrets—you have to clear that path. If that means taking responsibility for something, then take responsibility! You need a clear conscience to move toward your goals. Without a clear conscience, you will likely find ways to unconsciously sabotage yourself, because on some level you will not feel you deserve to have what you want in life.

> *"If you take responsibility for yourself you will develop a hunger to accomplish your dreams." ~ Les Brown ~*

**Teaching Responsibility**

In the last several years I have taught many real estate agents and real estate teams the value of taking responsibility. When you start your own business as an agent, you're often suddenly out of the comfort zone of your nine-to-five job and your regular paycheck. In spite of this, and before you sober up to your new reality, you think, "Oh great! I'm my own boss. I can do whatever I want." You wake up at 11:00 a.m. You get in the shower about 11:30, 12:00, you don't eat breakfast until 1:00 or 2:00. By the time you're on the phone, it's 3:00 p.m.; you're just starting your day and you're wondering why you have no business.

True story: I really want to own a gas station. I want to own an Arco station to be precise. This has been a dream of mine since I was a kid, basically because I grew up in a really poor family and never wanted my family to worry about running out of toilet paper or gas. Arco was economical, and the people who worked behind the counter were always friendly to my family, so I decided I wanted to own one when I grew up. Even to this day I only get my gas from Arco stations.

Using this as an example, I would ask the agents, "If somebody came along and gave you the keys to an Arco gas station right now, what would you do to get it to make money? How many hours would you work?"

And they would all say the same thing: "As many hours as it would take."

"But that doesn't make any sense. You're not going to work there 24 hours a day, so how many hours are you going to work?"

They would say that they were going to work there as many hours as they could, maybe even 80 hours a week.

"You're going to work 80 hours a week! For how long?"

"Until it's profitable."

"Well, what does that mean? What are you going to do?"

"I'm going to work on advertising. I'm going to look at my inventory. I'm going to look at pricing. I'm going to look at my connections and come up with a marketing strategy to compete with other gas stations in the area."

"All right, so you'd take responsibility for your business. You want to make a profit; you don't want to go into debt by having all this stuff sitting in your store that isn't selling because you're not taking your business seriously."

As a real estate agent (or any independent contractor), you have to do the same thing. You have to look in the mirror and be able to say to yourself, "I'm going to give this one hundred and ten percent. I'm going to give this everything I've got." Until you're willing to do that, you can't realistically expect to achieve your goal, whatever goal that is. How can you expect to achieve your goal if you're not willing to take responsibility for your actions and choices? You need to take responsibility for your day-to-day, hour-by-hour, minute-by-minute actions toward achieving those goals.

However, you must also remember that an essential aspect of taking responsibility for yourself and your goals is taking responsibility for your physical, mental, emotional, and spiritual health and well-being. Find the space and time to be with your family, to exercise, to eat well, to have fun, to meditate or pray, to have meaningful social interactions, to get enough sleep. These are all activities that will ultimately support you on your path to achieving your goals.

If you exhaust yourself, the time and energy you spend trying to achieve your goals won't get you very far very fast. Take responsibility for your own well-being in service to creating the life you want on every level.

> *"The willingness to accept responsibility for one's own life is the source from which self-respect springs." ~ Joan Didion ~*

**Taking Responsibility**

Taking responsibility for your situation is essential. Whether you're in a bad situation or a great situation, you have to look at responsibility on multiple levels. Let's start with a scenario where you're actually in a good place in your life but are yearning for a change. You like your job just fine, and you're earning enough, but you feel you need to make a change. It's simply time for you to do something different with your life.

Let's say you've decided it's time for you to go after your real dream of being a singer, or wrestler, or painter, or teacher. Or perhaps you've decided you really want to take a year off and travel the world. Before you quit your job, before you take the risk, you need to take responsibility for whatever your current situation is and think before you act. You want to make sure you're taking responsibility for your commitments to yourself and others, as well as to your own health and safety. Ask yourself, does quitting your job make sense? Will it help you achieve your goals? Does it put you or your loved ones and dependents in any kind of unnecessary jeopardy?

On the other hand, if you happen to be navigating a painful situation, one in which you perhaps do not feel you have a lot of choices—if you're going through a really bad breakup or have just lost your job—you may want to take a step back and see how, or if, you contributed to the situation. Take responsibility and own it. Why is this important? To move forward, you have to own your piece so you have a clear mind, a clear conscience, and a clear focus. You cannot effectively move toward your goals or update them without taking full responsibility for yourself—your behavior, your attitude, your actions, your words, and your participation. And you don't want to repeat the same mistakes.

> *"Somebody has to take responsibility for being a leader."*
>
> *~ Toni Morrison ~*

## Gerald Hankerson's Story

Gerald Hankerson and I have been friends for a long time, and I'm super proud of what he's accomplished and the example he sets for all people, particularly young people. He continues to demonstrate courage, strength, and perseverance in the face of personal and societal challenges. Here's his story, in his own words:

I'm the president of the NAACP for Seattle King County as well as the president of the NAACP for Alaska, Oregon, and Washington. In addition to that, I'm the director for policy development for the Washington Community Action Network, which is the largest grassroots organization in the state.

I grew up in Georgia. I was born a breech baby and was in the hospital for six months after I was born. When I was well enough to be released from the hospital, my mom didn't come to get me –she had disappeared – so I ended up living with foster families through my teen years. I eventually discovered that my mom was living in Seattle, and in 1987, when I was 17, I went to see her. By the time I was 18, I was charged with aggravated murder for assisting in a crime I did not commit.

I was convicted in Washington State in 1987 and sentenced to life in prison without the possibility of parole. I challenged the court system appeal after appeal after appeal and didn't get anywhere, but, in the process, I learned a lot about the legal system. In 2006, in my 23rd year in prison, I decided to file for clemency and applied for a pardon from the governor. I had a lot of community support because of the programs I was overseeing in prison. Influential people outside the prison took notice because, on behalf of the inmates, I took on the role of the prison liaison in order to bring awareness about our conditions to the outside world.

Getting involved in the prison programs was one of the things that kept me going while I was incarcerated. I loved being able to work with others, being able to help them. After I had been in prison about 10 years, I started to wake up. I took on the responsibility of helping other inmates because I noticed so many guys my age and younger coming into prison, getting out, and then coming back, like clockwork. I knew that if someone had stepped up to help educate me when I first entered prison, I might have had a different experience. I chose to spend my time doing whatever I could to make a miserable experience better for as many people as I could.

Miraculously, I got a unanimous recommendation from the Clemency Board to the governor saying I should be set free. Ten months later the governor turned me down. That really destroyed me. But the community came together and created a "Free Gerald Hankerson" coalition, which reached out to the governor and asked her to reconsider—and she did. On April 9, 2009, I became the first man in the history of Washington State to get out of prison after being sentenced to life.

When I got out I was involved in community activities. I remembered those people who were there for me during my appeals and who stood up for me when I applied for clemency. I was committed to those organizations, particularly the NAACP. After three years I'd moved up the ranks from just being a regular member to the position of vice president. I started out as a kid sitting in prison with no hope of ever getting out, and there I was, 23 years later, sitting in a room with governors and negotiating across the table with judges and lawyers. The next thing I knew, the president stepped down and I became president. My goal was and is to give back, to be involved and authentic. I'm looking out for the little people who don't have the opportunity to speak for themselves. I'm not afraid to speak truth to power because, after all, you can't do anything to me that hasn't already been done.

Nothing worth having ever comes easy. I haven't known anyone to be successful without some sort of struggle. To be successful you have to be able to embrace that, take responsibility for your life, persevere, and never give up.

\*\*\*

Clearly there are different levels of responsibility, such as apologizing for hurting someone or giving unsolicited forgiveness, and being accountable to yourself and your goals. And then there is the level of responsibility Gerald took on. He took responsibility for the welfare of others by being a mentor and a flesh-and-blood guardian angel. Because he recognized how valuable it would have been for him to have had someone show him the ropes when he first entered prison, he made himself available to prisoners who wanted his guidance and support.

His empathy and awareness led him to extend himself, and in so doing he gained the respect and assistance of people in positions of power who were able to help him. As the saying goes, "What goes around comes around." Gerald did not help others with an eye toward what he might get in return. But because he showed himself to be someone who was willing and able to take responsibility for others, he was seen and treated as a leader. Now working in the world in that role, he is helping, mentoring, and guiding more people all the time.

## But It's Not My Fault

I hear you...and maybe that's true. However, you are the only one responsible for your responses, your attitude, and your behavior. This is not to say there aren't situations in which you are being held hostage or victimized. However, some believe we choose all our experiences in life before we are born, and some believe in destiny or fate. No matter what your belief or life circumstance is, and no matter how you are being treated or where or how you live, what you hold inside your heart and mind is your choice (unless you are dealing with certain kinds of mental illness).

I am not in a position to speak to mental illness, so I will leave that conversation to the experts. I do absolutely acknowledge that there are people whose circumstances are extreme and truly painful and frightening. I also acknowledge that children do not necessarily have the defenses to protect themselves from abusive situations, and that childhood trauma has an impact on the way adults behave, think, and feel. So I understand it is not necessarily easy to take full responsibility for your life in every moment and on every level.

My wish is not to further shame you but to empower you with the radical idea that even if your life is painful, even if your freedom is curtailed, even if you are suffering from PTSD or other trauma-related issues, you have the ability to take full responsibility for your life right now in this moment. This does not mean letting those who have hurt you off the hook, submitting to an intolerable situation, refusing treatment for mental health issues, or blaming and chastising yourself. It means taking your life back—taking your thoughts and feelings back, taking your spirit back, and committing to loving yourself and moving forward as best you can.

As noted earlier in this chapter, taking responsibility can mean different things in different circumstances. It can mean making amends for something you have done to hurt someone else, it can mean forgiving those who have wronged you, it can mean fully accepting who you are as a composite of all you have experienced for better or worse, it can mean taking care of yourself on every level—mental, emotional, physical, spiritual—and it can mean taking care of those you have made a commitment to—your children, spouse, family, friends, co-workers, boss, clients, and so on.

What I'm talking about here encompasses all the various kinds of responsibility mentioned earlier, as well as the deepest, most essential level of responsibility a human being can engage in or commit to, and that is your responsibility to the core of who you truly are. What are your values? What do you love? If you can claim or reclaim your values, your love, no one can hurt you at your core. Your life may be difficult, but if you can take full responsibility for your authentic self, you have the means to create a different kind of life for yourself. Or at the very least, a way to be at peace with whatever you are having to live through right now.

Ultimately this self-acceptance, this commitment to your values, yourself, your spirit, will give you the strength and courage to face your situation and change it, if you so wish. You are more powerful than you can imagine, but you have to recognize that power before you can fully harness it. The only way to do that is to claim it by embracing total responsibility for all that you are and all that you have experienced. If you are blaming others, or circumstances, you are giving your power to something outside yourself, and that something outside yourself will never allow you to fully grow so long as you are committed to the idea that it has power over you.

Take your power back by taking full responsibility for your life!

> *"We are made wise not by the recollection of our past, but by the responsibility for our future."~ George Bernard Shaw ~*

## Exercises

Now it's your turn. Here are some questions and exercises to help you understand how and when to take responsibility:

1. Is there anyone in your life you feel you'd like to apologize to or from whom you'd like to ask forgiveness?

2. If there is, even if you don't feel you are ready to make reparations, write an apology letter to that person. If after you've written the letter you feel you'd like to present it to the person in question, feel free to do so.

3. Whether or not you give the letter to the person from who you're seeking forgiveness, ask yourself if you feel better, lighter, and clearer now that you've written it. If you do, bravo! If you do not, keep exploring your feelings of guilt, shame, regret, and remorse until you are able to have a deeper understanding of what you might do to shift those feelings.

4.  Have you taken full responsibility for yourself, your life, your family, and your goals? Make a list of the times in your life you feel you are out of integrity with your own values. Do you procrastinate? Do you tell white lies? Are you always just a little late? Do you cheat on your diet? Do you drink too much? Do you spend more money than you can afford? Do you put up with behavior from others that makes you uncomfortable because you don't like to confront them?

5.  Is there anything on your list you feel you'd be willing to change? What would it take to be on time, for instance? Practice taking responsibility for yourself.

6.  If you feel called to be of service to others, think about how you would like to be of assistance and to whom. Your sister might need a babysitter, or your son might need consistent help with his homework, or you might feel compelled to start working at a soup kitchen or join an organization dedicated to serving an underserved community. Service isn't mandatory, and it's only really effective if you feel genuinely called to serve. You are not a bad person for just handling your own life, and you

are not necessarily a good person because you help others. Helping others is most meaningful when it is an outgrowth of your own interests and concerns and when it doesn't take away from the time and energy you need to take care of yourself.

Always take care of yourself first and only extend yourself to others when you have the time, energy, and desire to do so.

**Remember:** The first **E** in **FREEDOM** stands for cultivating **Esteem** by owning your stuff.

# Chapter Seven

# Goals

*"Our goals can only be reached through a vehicle of a plan, in which we must fervently believe, and upon which we must vigorously act. There is no other route to success."*

*~ Pablo Picasso ~*

## Release Readiness

When I was in my 20s, the prison staff started paying attention to the books I was getting sent to me and I assume were thinking, *If anybody's mindset has changed, it has to be this guy's.* I was popular and had a good reputation, but I'd grown up in this prison and had been in trouble in the past. However, they could see a shift was happening and I was changing. After I had taken their class on preparing for release from prison, and written a several-page report on things I felt were missing, they asked me to teach a class called Release Readiness.

The first thing I would say in class was, "You have to change your mindset and reset yourself, and in order to change your mindset, you have to set some goals. You have to look into yourself and find out what you like to do. You don't have to do things you don't like to do. If you plan ahead for what you want to do, you can do it. You just need to have some goals."

You need to have a big goal that may seem unattainable, and then smaller goals that lead to that big goal. Maybe you never make it to the big goal, but you can find happiness and success achieving the smaller goals. But how do you determine what your goal is? Ask yourself these questions: What do I like to do? What am I called to do? What would give my life meaning or purpose? What would make me happy? As you start to get closer to what you really want to do with your life, or how you want your life to look or feel, begin to write down your goals and keep track of your progress toward those goals.

> *"I don't focus on what I'm up against.*
>
> *I focus on my goals and I try to ignore the rest."*
>
> *~ Venus Williams ~*

## Setting Goals

This is my favorite chapter because setting goals and changing your mindset to achieve them is what this book is about. Without goals we are stagnant and not really moving in any direction. Without goals we become complacent, just doing the same thing and engaged in the same routines, day in and day out, without a destination.

Before I get into my thoughts on goal setting, I want to turn you on to two tools that will help you set and achieve your goals. There is the fast and easy goal sheet I learned about from Keller Williams Realty called the 411, which I currently use for setting my own goals. Then there is a whole system I learned about in a book I call the "Goal-setting Bible." That book, by Mike Pettigrew, is actually titled *The*

*Most Powerful Goal Achievement System in the World.* These two tools are amazing for goal setting and tracking.

## The 411 Productivity Tool

Keller Williams provides educational tools they share with their Realtors to help them keep growing in their businesses. The 411 enables you to track your weekly, monthly, and yearly goals. By setting your yearly goal you can work backward to create your monthly goals and then understand what it will take weekly to accomplish your monthly and yearly goals. I have made it easy for you to go to the Keller Williams page, which will help you fully understand how to use the 411 and give you downloadable documents. Go to **411.res3t.com.**

## Goal-setting Bible

There is so much value in the book *The Most Powerful Goal Achievement System in the World.* Mike Pettigrew offers seven steps you can take to achieve your goals. Interestingly, steps six and seven are about taking action and mindset. Hmm... Sound familiar? His book shares a system that is really the foundation for all my goal setting today. I cannot recommend this book highly enough.

When establishing goals, it is extremely important to set deadlines. Without deadlines you have goals without accountability. The steps in his book give you tools for setting your goals and the timelines for those goals. I have a busy life and I get distracted fairly easily. These tools keep me on track and are not hard to apply. Before you know it, you will be on track to accomplishing the goals you set for yourself.

## More Thoughts on Goal Setting

The authors of *The 4 Disciplines of Execution* say that your chance of achieving two or three goals with excellence are high, but the more goals you try to juggle at once, the less likely you will be to reach them.

A good example of this is my friend Jay (not his real name). Every time I talk to him, he has a new side job. He invests money to get all the tools and all the stuff he needs for that new job. And then all that stuff goes in his garage. Then he studies and reads and sets another goal to do another type of side job. He gets the tools and the things he needs, and then that stuff gets stacked in the garage next to the other stuff. He never seems to be progressing in anything. Unfortunately, because of his inability to focus or apply himself to any one thing and move forward with his life, he went from having a nice house and family to losing his house and getting divorced.

If you're like me or my friend Jay, you have difficulty keeping your focus. Maybe you have ADD, maybe you see a lot of shiny objects that attract your attention. Maybe your mind is scattered like a bunch of squirrels every time you try to focus. Dr. Daniel Amen, author of *Change Your Brain, Change Your Life*, offers valuable advice for staying centered on your goals. He emphasizes being positive and creating a habit that will support your ability to stay committed and intentional. Losing focus is easy to do, especially when you are easily distracted. I have found Dr. Amen's tools for setting your intentions by writing down your goals to be excellent, and they have helped me reach my goals.

The following quote refers to his method for creating a list of your top goals and using the list to support your process of moving toward your goals:

> Write what you want, *not* what you don't want. Be positive and write in the first person. Keep a copy with you for several days so you can work on it over time. After you finish the initial draft (you'll want to update it frequently), place this piece of paper where you can see it every day, such as in your briefcase, on your refrigerator, by your bed, or on the bathroom mirror. In that way, every day you can focus your eyes on what's important to you. This makes it easier for you to supervise yourself and to match your behavior to get what you want. Your life will become more conscious, and you will spend your energy on goals that are important to you.

Another tool I've found quite helpful in staying focused and positive as I move toward my goals is the use of affirmations—short, positive statements in the first person that encourage and support you on every level. An affirmation can be something like: "I wake up every morning feeling energized and enthusiastic about my life!" Or, "Every day I am easily and joyfully moving closer to my goal of owning a home!"

Affirmations can cover every aspect of your life: both short- and long-term goals about relationships, health, finances, family, travel, etc. They are easy and fun to create and will immediately give you a boost of energy and a feeling of renewed confidence. Your affirmations aren't likely to work if they make you feel anxious, overwhelmed, or hopeless! If your affirmations don't make you feel happy, confident, and enthusiastic, rewrite them until they do.

Pat Hiban, who wrote *6 Steps to 7 Figures*, has some helpful thoughts about why and how to use affirmations: "I also learned the power of making affirmations to myself. And after a few years I ramped this up by making it a habit. Sometimes I wrote them down... Now I record them on my phone and replay them whenever I get a chance. Ninety percent of the affirmations I've made over the years have come true. Typically about half come true the year I make them and the rest come true within five years or so."

\*\*\*

Goals are the foundation for everything. You cannot build a house before you put the foundation down. To accomplish your goals, you need to have good habits and discipline, and be dedicated and focused. You also need to set realistic goals. So, is it realistic to say you want to be a millionaire? The answer is yes, but you need to believe in yourself. You need to believe in yourself because if you don't, how do you expect anybody else to believe in you? All goals will inevitably involve networking with other people to get there, so you have to believe in yourself.

If you're going to make a change in your life, you eventually need to know what your goal is. You will need to do some deep thinking or soul searching to figure out what you want. When you think you've discovered what you want to pursue, how do you know whether your goals are really *your* goals? That might seem obvious, but a lot of people do what their parents think they should do, and they're not conscious that they're doing that until they get into it and realize they hate it. How do you connect with what's authentic to you?

To answer this question I'll tell you a story instead of giving you a dissertation on how to pick a goal: I love computers. In prison, I'd built a network, web pages, a database, and they all worked together so that students could log in and communicate on a closed-circuit network. It's called a LAN or local area network. It's not the Internet, which we were not allowed to have access to. I used the LAN to create a database that stored all the students' grades and scores for all the chapter work. Then I created a website for them to log in to that showed where they were in the course and what their grades were. That sounds super easy, but it took a long time and I taught myself. Nobody taught me how to do it. I had to learn it and teach myself.

My computer skills are what ultimately got me recruited by another mortgage company and gave me my highest paying job—$60,000 a year. It was a big deal to me. I went from minimum wage to $60,000 per year. I was a very happy guy. I'd never seen that much money! My work partner was an older woman who wasn't patient; she just wanted to do her job and go home. She didn't have a teacher's heart. I got laid off from that job six months in. I wasn't picking up what they needed me to because she wasn't making time to teach me. So it was frustrating.

However, before I got laid off, I knew I wasn't happy. I would think to myself, *Is this really what I'm going to be doing for the rest of my life?* I could feel my unhappiness and doubt when I woke up; I could feel those feelings when I was on my way to work. I was making good money—that was the part that made me happy—but I wasn't feeling good. It wasn't really what I wanted to do.

Of course, it turned out that being laid off was a gift, because it would have been hard to quit a job that paid so well. Not long after I was laid off, a friend called me and helpfully reminded me that I'd always wanted to get into real estate. That had always been my true goal. I was getting to the end of my unemployment money, so I had to make a decision about what I would do next.

With encouragement from the girlfriend I had at that time, I signed up for a real estate license course. She kept saying, "You can do it, you can do it, you can do it..." I was grateful and excited, but I also knew I could be lazy at times. So I went into the bathroom and looked in the mirror and asked myself, "Are you going to give it a hundred percent?" I stood there and stared at myself for a minute or two and then asked, "Are you that committed? Is this for you?"

I felt a surge of extreme clarity. My mind and body were in sync and I said out loud, "I'm going to do this. I'm going to give it a hundred and fifty percent and I'm going to kill it. I'm going to make this dream happen!" I walked out of the bathroom, sat down with my girlfriend, and said, "All right, I'm in, and I'm not going to give up!"

She was amazingly supportive and probably could've passed that test too because of how much time she studied with me. She believed in me because I believed in myself. She believed in me because I was all in. I would work all day, come home, and study for hours at night. I took the practice tests over and over again until I knew the material cold. Nothing was going to keep me from my goal!

It wasn't like I didn't doubt myself, because I did. My inner naysayer was always talking to me. I took and failed the test two times before I passed it. Each failure crushed me because I had been studying so hard every night. Every day. Then boom! I didn't pass. So I would be down and stressed out for a while, but my goal was always right there in front of me, pushing me. My support system was there for me, pushing me. So I pushed on and on. Then BAM! I passed the exam! I was so excited to achieve that goal. I remember that day like it was yesterday. I was so happy, and my mind and body felt joy in that moment to have accomplished a goal I had set and had been working toward for years. What a feeling! It was AMAZING and it is a feeling you can experience too!

> *"Faith is the ability to see the invisible,*
>
> *believe in the incredible,*
>
> *in order to receive what the masses think is impossible."*
>
> *~ Buddha ~*

**Tarra's Story**

When I think of what it takes to accomplish major goals, I think of my friend Tarra. While working to help people change their lives, I often get the opportunity to partner with very cool organizations and meet amazing people. One of those cool organizations is Civil Survival, where Tarra works as executive director. In spite of a life filled with struggle, Tarra was ultimately able to reset her mind and focus on achieving some incredible goals. I have endless admiration for her. Here is what Tarra had to say about her journey:

I was born into a family where everybody suffered with drug addiction and had been incarcerated. I grew up in poverty, came from a broken family. My parents divorced when I was a year old. I experienced a lot of trauma as a child. I was sexually abused as early as 11 years old. I eventually left home at 13 and lived on the streets where I was further traumatized. I became a mom at 14 and was homeless. That was actually a blessing for me because when I got pregnant I wanted my son to have a different life than I had, so I went back to high school and finished four years of work in two. I graduated at 16, went straight into nursing school, got my bachelor's degree in nursing, and bought a home. I was 22 and I thought I'd escaped the patterns in my family, but I never really dealt with the underlying trauma of my childhood. And so eventually I ended up using drugs, became addicted, and went to prison for dealing. I was selling drugs to support my habit.

In prison I finally had time to start healing. I worked the NA steps and became open about my trauma and the reasons I used drugs. I began to really heal from those early childhood experiences that caused me to carry so much shame, and I started to break free from that shame. When I was released from prison, nobody would give me a job because of my criminal history. So I was working at Burger King even though I had a bachelor's degree in nursing. I had other legal issues coming up and I had legal financial obligations (which is the court fines that everybody gets as part of a criminal conviction in Washington state.), and the interest that had accrued on those. My house went into foreclosure when I was in prison, and when I went back home, I got evicted because the mortgage hadn't been paid for a while.

My husband divorced me while I was in prison, and I couldn't respond to him because I didn't have the court forms to do so. So all my consumer debt went into collections, and I had to file bankruptcy. I had all these legal issues, but I was fortunate to get legal help when I needed it. Not everybody does. These lawyers not only helped me with these issues, but offered me some humanity and encouraged me, mentored me, and even told me I should go to law school. But I thought, *I can't go to law school, I have six felonies. There's no way I can do that.* Then somebody told me about a book called *Law Man* by Shon Hopwood, who robbed five banks and served 12 years in federal prison.

In January 2014 I read his book in two days, and then contacted Shon through Facebook. He was in his second year of law school at the University of Washington. I met with him at the university and he was really an inspiration to me to start this journey of becoming a lawyer. Shon and I became friends, and he helped me write my personal statement for my application to law school.

I got accepted to Seattle University Law School and started there in August 2014. During my time I networked continuously, signed up for every organization and coalition meeting—anything. The governor ultimately appointed me to two different boards, and I'm now the co-chair of the statewide reentry council. My passion has always been to help other people reenter the world after prison because I was so lucky to get help when I needed it. I wanted to be a lawyer to help former prisoners with their legal issues. There are things I could do for them as a lawyer: get their financial obligations waived, help them reunite with their kids, defend them in an eviction, and help them file bankruptcy.

During law school I worked super hard and graduated magna cum laude. I got the Dean's Medal, which is given every year to one student who shows their commitment to social justice. I also got a Skadden Fellowship, which law students have been applying to receive for 30 years. I'm the first person in my school to get it. This fellowship mostly goes to the folks from the top 10 law schools in the country: Harvard, Yale, Stanford, etc. It provided me with a salary for two years to do the project of my dreams: to help individuals with their barriers to reentry by representing them in court while also working to change the system with policy reform.

Then I applied to sit for the bar exam, but the Washington State Bar Association Character and Fitness Board denied my application, saying that because of my past convictions I could not sit for the bar exam. I was devastated. That was April 14, 2017. It was really painful because Shon Hopwood went through that board and got a unanimous approval. I have other friends who had criminal histories who were able to take that test too, and also friends who were denied like I was. It seems there is no objective standard of why and how they were making these decisions.

So I chose to appeal this decision. My original attorney, John Strait, got Shon Hopwood involved in my case because Shon is now a Georgetown University law professor and a brilliant appellate attorney. We appealed to the state Supreme Court. I had so much support from organizations like the ACLU. A total of 48 organizations across the country and 54 new attorneys signed on to the brief in addition to the hundred that had already written letters in my initial application. So we had a powerful case before the Supreme Court.

My oral argument hearing was on November 16, 2017. It was standing room only and even the lobby was filled. They had to bring in an extra TV for the overflow in the lobby. The most amazing thing was that generally it takes months to get a decision from the state Supreme Court, but this time they had a decision within hours—and ruled unanimously in my favor! Within hours! I took the bar exam February 27 and 28, 2018, and passed! On June 16 I got sworn in!!!

It was hard at times, but I had to keep coming back to the bigger goal for motivation and inspiration: this isn't just for me and my clients, this is for my children too, so we can have a future. They can have a happy mom who's doing work she's passionate about and who also provides for the family. So I had to keep coming back to these bigger goals and my vision of changing the system. I am a person of faith, and I really feel like God has put me here for a particular purpose. To be doing this work makes me feel proud and builds my self-esteem. I'm helping other people and helping my family at the same time. These goals were always what kept me persevering through the hard work.

Pick a goal that is driven internally in some way—something you're passionate about. You have to have that internal drive to succeed. And if you don't have that internal drive to succeed, then you will likely not. Any goal worth having comes with challenges.

*** 

Tarra's experience absolutely supports her advice to pick a goal that is internally driven. In other words, a goal that is authentic to you, not a goal that someone else has chosen for you, not a goal you think you *should* accomplish, but a goal that feeds your soul—a goal that will allow you to move toward your deepest desires, highest ideals, and most persistent dreams. It is my sincere belief that if you head in the direction of *your* dreams, you will experience a much greater sense of satisfaction than if you temper your dreams and goals to fit someone else's expectations, or out of your own fear of failing.

You cannot fail in the pursuit of your authentic goals and desires. You may experience what feels like setbacks or obstacles, but from my perspective, setbacks and obstacles are actually opportunities for you to redirect your focus and to continue to revise and update your goals as you move toward them. Your authentic drive will not misdirect you. It may take you longer than you want to get to your destination, but everything you learn along the way will ultimately enrich your life.

> *"We are the creative force of our life, and through our own decisions rather than our conditions, if we carefully learn to do certain things, we can accomplish those goals."*
>
> *~ Stephen Covey ~*

## Create a Life You Love Now!

I intentionally didn't call this section, "Create the Life of Your Dreams Now!" That's because, regardless of your intention, commitment, focus, vision, action steps, networking, etc., it is possible that your goals and dreams may change as you move forward, or your goals may manifest in a form that looks a little or even vastly different than you'd imagined. I'm not saying this to discourage you—quite the opposite. I know you will create a life you love if you pursue your heartfelt goals with dedication, faith, belief, and the willingness to shift your course when necessary.

---

*"You reap what you sow 100% of the time."*

~ *Pat Hiban,* 6 Steps to 7 Figures ~

---

**Exercises**

Here are questions and exercises to help you start formulating your goals:

1. Make a list of your most cherished goals, even if they seem too big or unattainable. If your goals are at least 50% believable, there is a good chance you will be able to achieve them. As Pat Hiban writes in *6 Steps to 7 Figures*, "Clearly, having a tangible, written reminder of your goal really works, because it constantly reminds you of what you're striving to achieve." Sit with this list for a few days.

2. If you can't come up with a list of goals, think about what you loved to do as a child, what you thought you wanted to be when you grew up. Do any of these early dreams still resonate? If not, what do you love doing now? What are your hobbies and interests? Do you know anyone with a career or lifestyle you secretly (or not so secretly) envy or admire? If you are still coming up with a blank, start researching careers and people with lifestyles that

seem appealing. Compile a list of *possible* goals. You can always revise later. In fact, you can keep revising this list for the rest of your life. Even if you feel like you know exactly what you want, you may find that you will need to revise your goals at some point in your process of moving toward them.

3. After you have allowed yourself to feel drawn into your most cherished dreams and goals, pick your top three and write a paragraph or two beneath each one in which you describe what you think your life will be like if you achieve that goal.

4. After you have done this, ask yourself whether your number one goal is still number one. If it is, great! If it isn't, rearrange your list.

5. Now, write an expanded vision (maybe a page or two) of what your life would be like if you achieved your number one goal. Notice how you feel. Do you feel excited and energized, or insecure and cynical?

6. If you are feeling uncomfortable emotions when you imagine achieving your dream, pay attention to these feelings and ask yourself why you are feeling this way.

Is it perhaps because this isn't truly your number one goal in life? Or is it because it feels unattainable?

7. Explore your feelings and revise your goals as needed.

8. When you are clear about the goal you are most interested in pursuing now, you may want to begin using various manifestation and visualization tools to further refine your goal and create the opportunity for it to begin to manifest in your life. Vision boards are fun to create (you will find clear instructions online for creating one if you don't know what I'm referring to). Continuing to expand and refine your page-long vision is a great way to generate energy, excitement, and motivation. Writing affirmations (you can also find instructions online for doing this) can be empowering and motivating. Explore, refine, and energize your goals, but most of all, HAVE FUN!

**Remember:** The second **E** in **FREEDOM** stands for **Educate** yourself and **Enumerate** your goals.

# <u>Chapter Eight</u>

# Action

*"Faith is taking the first step even when*

*you don't see the whole staircase."*

*~ Martin Luther King Jr. ~*

**Reading Everything**

When I first started thinking about what I wanted to do with my life, I realized I didn't have the same skills or interests that a lot of guys in prison have or develop. I didn't have the experience of an electrician or plumber, and I couldn't do carpentry, but I was good at computer work and I was good at selling stuff and hustling (my mom used to tell me I could sell ice to Eskimos). I realized I needed to do something different to prepare for my release. I set a goal to change my mindset from living the day-to-day prison existence of playing poker, doing nothing, and working out, to preparing for a fulfilling, successful, and prosperous life outside of prison. This goal of finding something I enjoyed and would be successful doing motivated me to begin reading and studying.

Naturally, I looked for books on topics that interested me. Before I found my first title, I decided that if I liked a book, I would read all of that author's books before moving on to any other subject or author. I'm not sure what title grabbed my attention first, but it was a book by Robert Shemin that started my journey toward becoming a real estate broker years later. It was a great book, so I read all of his books. (Figures that the author of the first book I picked up happened to have written 15 books! Not one or two but 15! Really?) After I finished all his books, I read every real estate book I could get my hands on. (Take a look at the back cover of this book. Robert Shemin read *my* book and wrote a great review to encourage people to read it! How AWESOME is that!)

> *"We are what we repeatedly do. Excellence, then,*
>
> *is not an act, but a habit."*
>
> *~ Will Durant ~*

## Taking Action

The difference between coping and taking action is your mindset. Coping is being in the moment, being in acceptance, and relieving stress, whereas taking action involves moving forward toward an outcome. This outcome may be nebulous or a clearly defined goal. In other words, your action steps may be exploratory, or specifically designed to get you exactly where you know you want to be. Either way, your action steps will move you forward and give you information about where you're going, what additional actions you will need to do to get there, and whether you will have to adjust your timeframe, expectations, or ultimate goal.

Most people take action toward an outcome every day. Because of that, action steps may not be noticed for what they are—deliberate and incremental steps toward an outcome or goal. For instance, suppose you get up on a sunny Saturday morning and decide you want to take your family to the zoo. What steps would you have to take to make that happen? Perhaps you fix breakfast for your family, take a shower, get dressed, make sure you have the directions, round up your crew, gas up the car, and when you get there, buy tickets and figure out what everyone wants to do, and when and where you will eat lunch, etc. All the steps you take to get yourself and your family to the zoo lead you to being able to achieve your goal.

Even though the steps may have been relatively easy, if not mundane, you probably had a great time at the zoo and even a feeling of accomplishment. You decided to go to the zoo, but you didn't actually realize what it would take to get there because you just did it. You made the decision to go and you figured out what you had to do each step of the way to make it happen. It actually took a chain of events you were hyper-focused on in order to get there. And this has probably happened millions of times in your life—every day you decide to do something, you get hyper-focused on making it happen, and more often than not it does. You go to work, you go to the movies, you make dinner, you take a vacation, etc. The energy and the focus you put into the action steps you take every day to accomplish the immediate goals you have in your life require the same energy and focus you would apply to accomplishing major life-changing goals.

The action steps you would take to discover your ultimate goal or goals will most likely be of a different nature than the steps you would take to achieve a clearly defined goal. Exploratory action steps may lead you down a variety of paths and may prompt you to backtrack or start over, but you must be as focused on these sorts of action steps as you would be on those you might take to get into medical school, or get a specific job, or write your memoir. Remember that action steps are by their nature small steps, one foot in front of the other.

However, you should be aware of the "paralysis of analysis." This happens when you look at your desired outcome, your future, or your goals and start to research and study them and research and study them and research and study them but don't take action. You just keep analyzing everything and taking notes but never start to *do* anything. Don't get stuck in analysis paralysis by analyzing the big picture for too long. Be sure to always be taking the next step necessary to move forward.

It is obvious that you must take action to create anything in life; however, I have encountered people who believe they are taking action when they are simply daydreaming or fantasizing about what they want. You will not become a billionaire by lying around watching the TV show *Billions* on Netflix. It may be inspiring, which is a good thing, but you will ultimately have to get off the couch and do something if you are expecting to generate that kind of wealth. So, what are you going to do? Research, read, interview billionaires, hire a wealth coach, learn about the stock market—and take action based on what you've discovered and learned!

If you want to become a yoga instructor and run your own studio, what do you do? Get in shape, take a yoga teacher training program, intern, get a position as a yoga teacher, research yoga businesses to understand what it takes to own and run a studio, etc.

What if you don't know what you want to do, but you love animals and know you want to work with them in some capacity. Figure out what kinds of animals you prefer working with. Volunteer at the ASPCA. Get work on a farm, or at a horse stable, or in a pet store, or at a veterinary office. Read, research, interview people who work with animals. Perhaps you will decide you want to become a dog trainer or a veterinarian.

Or...perhaps you want to become a mixed martial arts (MMA) fighter...

**Brandon's Story**

I recently had the opportunity to talk with my dedicated friend, Brandon. His journey is a great example of how to reset your mind and use all the principles in this book. Brandon tells the story of his path to becoming an MMA fighter and outlines the action steps he took along the way to achieving his goals. Here is Brandon's story as he tells it:

My name is Brandon, and I fight amateur MMA but will eventually be professional. I teach Brazilian jiu-jitsu to kids and adults and spend most of my time doing martial arts. Ever since I was a kid I had an interest in martial arts, but I was never really good at staying dedicated to anything. However, when I turned 12 I joined the Army Cadets just to start doing something. I didn't want to be a fat kid forever, and I figured that was a good way for me to get exercise. I learned a lot about discipline and fitness, and I enjoyed it. I switched high schools in grade nine and met this dude who was into MMA and weight lifting. I wasn't in cadets anymore and I needed something else to do, so we worked out together. He was a brown belt in judo and introduced me to martial arts. I eventually got into Korean-Brazilian jiu-jitsu.

I figured I'd learn jiu-jitsu first and then compete in some jiu-jitsu tournaments, and then start boxing and do a boxing match, and then start kickboxing and do a kickboxing match, and just kind of build myself up from there. By doing it that way, I was able to slowly get used to the idea of competing and fighting. I hadn't really competed in anything as a kid. Ultimately it worked and I started fighting.

As I started getting more and more focused, I decided to write down the action steps I needed to take to achieve my goals. The more I focused, the more specific I got. I would write down the 10 things I really wanted to accomplish in a particular year and carry my list around with me in my wallet. I read a Napoleon Hill book and he said you need to write out your goals every single day. If you don't have five minutes to write out your 10 goals for the year every day, do you really even have time to achieve those 10 goals? If you can't make the time to write them down, what are the chances that you're going to make the time to actually go out and achieve them?

Now they're in a training journal I carry with me. I write them out and then I'll write about what I did that day in training. I like to keep a checklist of all the steps I take every day to reach my goals, and schedule my days around those goals. My hours at work are affected by what my plans are. I used to work five days a week, but then I realized I wasn't getting enough kickboxing time in. So I told my boss I needed to leave earlier on Wednesdays because I wanted to start sparring. Now I get off early every Wednesday so I can go spar. I can kind of choose my hours. I'm not providing for anyone but myself, so I'm totally willing not to have a lot of money, and work just enough to pay my bills.

I knew I wanted to be an MMA fighter, so I started with jiu-jitsu. Once I started getting comfortable there, I thought to myself, *Okay, well, what's my next step?* I just take little steps each time. You need to have steps that lead you to your goal or your plan will never come true.

***

At the time of this interview, Brandon had just won a championship belt, which was a major goal and achievement for him. Changing your mindset can sometimes be a challenging journey, but if you are determined and follow the basic principles in this book, you will be able to reset your mind and create a life you love. As Pat Hiban writes in *6 Steps to 7 Figures*, "Whatever it is that you do want to achieve—whether you want to climb a mountain or lead the next space shuttle, or you simply want to be a better employee, a better boss, or a more successful business owner, make more money, or be a better husband or wife or parent or friend—you need only to have the sheer determination to do it."

---

> *"Go for it now. The future is promised to no one."*
>
> *~ Wayne Dyer ~*

---

**Will Little's Story**

Will is a good friend who has a powerful and inspiring story to tell about achieving great success against all odds. Here is his story in his own words:

My mother left my father and we moved with my aunts and my three older sisters from North Carolina to Philadelphia when I was about a year old. My mother was 15 when she married my father, and they had four children together, so she was only 20 when she had me. My father wasn't present in my life, and as I grew up I began to wonder who was going to teach me how to become a man. I thought about it a lot. I was a reserved child. I was always quiet and observed everything. We moved often, so everywhere I went I had to make new friends and get comfortable with the environment and another school. We got robbed a few times, and I got to a point where I felt I had to protect my sisters and my mom. I was the only man in the house.

One incident that changed the course of my life was when my mom got into a fight with her boyfriend. I was 13 and decided to jump into the fight. He grabbed me, threw me against the wall, and put a gun in my face. I just stared at him. I wasn't afraid; it made me really angry and I kind of blacked out.

I wanted to help ease my mom's financial burdens, so I eventually ended up hustling—selling drugs on the street. It seemed easy at first because I thought there would be no consequences, but then I started getting into arguments with the guys in the neighborhood who were jealous because I was making more money. Eventually I wound up in a shootout and got arrested and charged with aggravated assault. I spent the next 10 years in prison.

My girlfriend was two weeks pregnant when I got locked up. She was 16 going on 17 and I was 19. When my son was born I decided I didn't want him to grow up the way I had, without a father. But for me to be a good father, I had to learn how to become a man. I had to learn what a man was. I knew I was going to change my life, and I knew I had to do it then and there, and I knew it would be an extreme transformation. I had to learn how to handle my anger. I often had extreme responses to provocation. If you spit on me I was going to punch you; if you punched me I was going to shoot you. I knew that the first thing I had to do was educate myself, because I'd dropped out of high school. So I went about getting my GED. I started studying and reading a little more.

I knew I had to deal with things differently and get a whole new perspective on myself, my life, and what I wanted for my son, and what I wanted for my future. I was determined. I really wanted to challenge myself to see if I could change. I challenged myself to learn. I figured learning new things would bring new outcomes. I started challenging my anger and trying to talk things out and communicate well. I also worked on cultivating empathy because everybody has emotions, everybody has problems.

I reverted back to the strengths I had as a child—what was innately in me, like my creativity and my thinking process, all the things I lost in the streets. I forgave myself and the other people who harmed me or my family members, and that allowed me to reinvent myself and grow into the person I am today. While I was in prison I started teaching the young men who had the same dilemmas, the same problems, the same issues I did. I was holding myself accountable even more because now they looked up to me. I developed my communication skills and opened myself up to them.

I recently wrote a book because I wanted to leave a legacy for my children, grandchildren, and great-grandchildren. I want them to know about the struggles I went through. I want them to know where they came from so they understand they can do anything. It took me six months to do the writing. I dedicated an hour a day after work to writing, and then I self-published through Amazon. It was therapeutic—reflecting on my life and revisiting those days and those times and the things that happened to me in my life. I talked about my pain and my family—my mother and father.

My book is called *ICY*, which is an acronym for Inner City Youth. It's not about glorifying street life or prison, but about looking into the real issues and what it's like to grow up around a lot of negativity. It's about self-evaluation and transformation. It's about following your dreams and your passion and actually carrying it out and living it out and becoming the best version of yourself.

\*\*\*

Through deeply honest self-examination, courage, focus, and determination, Will was able to radically reset his life path. His honest self-assessment allowed him to get clarity about what mattered to him, which in turn gave him the drive to create goals and take the necessary steps to achieve his goals. I'm deeply awed and inspired by this man and hope you are too. When you approach your life with honesty, courage, and commitment to your values and ideals, combined with step-by-step actions, you will not only reach your goals, but also find a level of purpose you would never have discovered if you hadn't challenged yourself to change your life, as Will did.

> *Every day you and I wake up, we face the same universal challenge: to overcome mediocrity and live to our full potential. It's the greatest challenge in human history—to rise above our excuses, do what's right, give our best and create the level 10 life we truly want—the one with no limits, the one so few people ever get to live.*
>
> ~ *Hal Elrod,* The Miracle Morning ~

**Just Do It!**

Easy to say, you might be thinking. But how do I know what to do or if what I'm planning to do will help me accomplish my goals. What if I'm just wasting my time? I'm here to tell you that *nothing* you do that is a potential step toward the realization of your dreams is ever a waste of your time. You may discover that a certain step or series of steps have not led you in the direction you wanted, or have even led you to an impasse, but if you are sincerely focused on your goals, you will find that in time the reason you took a seemingly unproductive step will be revealed. It may simply be a way for you to reevaluate your process or even your goal, or it may lead you someplace unexpected that creates new opportunities more in alignment with your deepest values and desires.

Trust your instincts. Follow the path you have set for yourself until that path gives you the clues you need to move in a different direction or to get more clarity about what you actually want. No energy is ever wasted that is spent in the honest pursuit of your dreams!

---

*"Success seems to be connected with action. Successful*

*people*

*keep moving. They make mistakes, but they don't quit."*

*~ Conrad Hilton ~*

---

## Exercises

Here are some questions and exercises to help you understand how and when to take action:

1. Look at the number one goal you settled on in the exercise from the last chapter. Without too much thought, jot down a list of all the various actions you might take to get closer to that goal—both long-range and immediate actions. You don't have to organize them yet, just get them down on paper.

2. After you've made this list, start to organize the action steps into long-range, shorter-range, and more immediate steps. Then break those lists down into steps you might take in the next week, in the next month, in the next three months, in the next six months, in the next year, in the next two years. and so on. This process will help you determine how long you think it might take you to reach your goal. Some goals might be accomplished in six months to a year; others may take 10 or more years.

3. After you've broken your action steps down into time frames, look at the steps you could take immediately and

ask yourself if you are willing and ready to begin moving toward your goal. If you are, then take action!

4. If you are not ready, start exploring the possible reasons for your reluctance. Are the steps doable? Are you asking yourself to do too much all at once? In other words, do you feel overwhelmed? (If so, perhaps you haven't broken down the bigger tasks or projects into smaller actions. Ask yourself, "What's the next action I need to take?") Or, are you reconsidering your goal? This is an opportunity for deeper exploration. You do *not* have to feel discouraged if you are hesitating. Your hesitation is an opportunity for you to continue to research, refine, and realign.

5. If you were not able to come up with a goal in the previous chapter, go ahead and make a list of action steps that will support you in discovering your goal. In fact, you can make that your goal for the time being—to discover your goals.

6. The most important step is to have fun. Allow yourself to explore, discover, dream, revise, ponder, research,

learn. This is a process, and there is no one way to get to your goal.

**Remember:** The **D** in **FREEDOM stands for** employing **Discipline** in the **Doing**.

# Chapter Nine

# Risk

*"The person who risks nothing does nothing,*

*has nothing, is nothing, and becomes nothing.*

*He may avoid suffering and sorrow, but he simply cannot*

*learn and feel and change and grow and love and live."*

~ Leo F. Buscaglia ~

**Old Country Buffet and Beyond**

When I was first released from prison, I went into what is called a work release program. I lived in Bellingham, Washington, in a regular house and worked in the community but was still under the jurisdiction of the prison. I got a job as a dishwasher at Old Country Buffet. I worked really hard and was told by a visiting manager named Jon Evans that I was the best dishwasher in the world! After my time there was up, I went to live with my aunt in a different part of the state. I didn't have a job, so within a few days of my arrival I started looking for something.

A mortgage company was looking for a real estate processor, and though I didn't know about the financing of real estate, I knew everything else about real estate, plus I had computer skills. When I read a description of the work a processor does, I thought, *I can do that work.* If you're in the mortgage business, then you know how WRONG I really was! I applied and got an interview.

When I told my aunt I was going to this job interview, she asked, "Why aren't you going to Burger King or McDonald's or something like that? You just came from Old Country Buffet." I had read so many self-help books that I understood she was making a naysayer comment that really had nothing to do with me, but was a reflection of her own limiting beliefs. I didn't let it affect me whatsoever. I said, "I'll give this a shot and maybe two other types of jobs a shot. And if I get them, cool. If I don't, then maybe I'll look at Burger King and McDonald's as options."

I managed to get an interview with the owners of the branch, Michael Tutty and his wife, Mary. They looked at my resume and saw my 270 college credits. (The approximate number of credits required to get a bachelor's degree is 120.) Michael asked, "Where did you go to school?" I thought, *I've got to take a risk here, because it's going to come out eventually.* There's no way a 14-year-old kid goes to prison for as long as I did and never has the truth of his circumstances come out. I felt I had to be open about myself and my background.

I said, "Here's the thing, I have a crazy life story."

Michael leaned back in his chair, propped his chin on his fist, and said, "I'm listening."

I told him my life story from foster care and the crime to prison. I actually told the story of the crime—the full story. It was a risk I had to take. I then pulled out a list with 100 books on it. Those were all the real estate books I'd read while I was in prison. Michael was impressed and offered to create a job for me in his company since he knew I wasn't going to be processor material.

He said, "You're not qualified for that job, but I'm going to make a position for you here. Your drive and dedication and what you've done in your life is amazing. I want to help you on your journey."

That moment was about taking a risk, and having the confidence to take a risk. I knew when I went in and he started asking me questions that I needed to accept my situation and take a risk—being open and honest about where I was, who I was as a person, and what I had done to get to that moment. I had prepared myself for that moment for years, and despite where I'd come from, I was a good fit.

Taking risks can sometimes be scary. Make sure they are planned-out risks, not irrational or spur-of-the-moment impulses. Unplanned, reckless risks can send you backward instead of the direction you are trying to go.

> *"The fishermen know that the sea is dangerous and the storm terrible, but they have never found these dangers sufficient reason for remaining ashore.."*
>
> *~ Vincent van Gogh ~*

**Taking Risks**

When it comes to setting major life-changing goals, eventually you're going to have to consider risk. Yes. Risk is necessary in every single situation. There are two types of risks: calculated risks and extreme risks. Before you take a risk, it's important to think it through. It should not be impulsive. Your mind and body have to be together, in alignment with each other, because if they're not, you're always going to second-guess yourself. You're always going to wonder whether you're doing the right thing.

You have to be dedicated to your goal and believe in it because there are going to be hard times and you're going to have to rely on that dedication to keep moving forward. If you're always feeling a conflict or if you're feeling unsure or uncertain, if your mind and your body are not together when you take a risk, you potentially put yourself in unnecessary jeopardy.

> *"Risks may make you win, or they will make you learn.*
>
> *Either of the benefits is worth daring for."*
>
> *~ Israelmore Ayivor ~*

**Kym's Story**

Kym has worked in the medical field for 17 years and recently decided to quit her job and go back to school for accounting. I'll let her tell her own story:

I got into the medical field because, to be honest, it was a short course and I didn't want to go to school for too long. I'm leaving because of poor management and low morale. There's no appreciation. After 10 years of service, all they gave me was a pin. In addition to the unsupportive work environment, there were never any supplies. If you're going to take blood, you need to have supplies to do that. The whole operation was just really poorly run.

I tried to stick it out because of my pension. It was really hard for me to walk away from that, but it came down to whether I was willing to jeopardize my happiness. After all, you only have one life, and life is precious. I would rather be happy than anything else. I started looking into different things to do because I was feeling anxious about going to work; I really didn't want to be there. I thought about what other options I had and started thinking about becoming a paramedic, but it was too much of the same thing. I wanted to do something completely different. And then I met somebody who was in the accounting course I ended up taking. When I met this person, I thought, *Oh my God, this is what I'm supposed to be doing.*

Now my car payment and my rent come out of my savings. But in spite of the temporary financial setback, it seems like everything is falling perfectly into place for me. I'm in school now and I'm loving it. I don't have anxiety anymore. I feel very much at peace.

***

Kym's story is so inspiring to me because it demonstrates the power of honoring your inner knowing. Kym allowed her anxiety to be her intuitive guide. She listened to the part of herself that wanted to be happy, not just secure. This is not to say security isn't important, but taking a calculated risk means you weigh the pros and cons of the various options in front of you and, after careful consideration, decide to make a leap of faith.

Kym knew right away that the risk she took was the right move because she experienced what she described as "everything...falling perfectly into place." This is often the payoff for having the courage to take a risk. A risk is an act of faith, and it requires some part of you to be willing to let go of the need to control every step of your journey and especially your need to control the outcome. A risk is a risk because there is no guarantee it will work out as you want. But a risk is worth taking when you weigh the pros and cons and find you are willing to let go of what you have now in the hope that you will be able to accomplish what you truly want down the line.

> *Pearls don't lie on the seashore.*
>
> *If you want one, you must dive for it.*
>
> *~ Chinese proverb ~*

**Philip Triem's Story**

Pondering risks and success made me think of my friend Philip's story. When I reached out to him, he was happy to share his experiences:

I come from a blue-collar background. It was definitely a dysfunctional home; my father was an alcoholic. There was a lot of chaos, a lot of violence. I always felt kind of inadequate and out of place. As I got older, I struggled with drug addiction and alcoholism myself. I've been to very dark places in my life, places I never wish anybody to go to. By the time I was 20 I'd been through five treatment centers and was locked up in the hospital a number of times.

So I got into the recovery culture for a while, but later stumbled in my early 30s and then once again connected to that community. It's been 15 years now, and in that period I discovered I just wanted freedom. I wanted to be able to have the life I'd always dreamed of and never had before. So I got into the corporate world, into the auto industry, where I was a finance director for many, many years. I loved the business, I loved the excitement, but I've always been the kind of guy who wants more, better, and different.

In the auto industry I got really good at negotiating with banks. That was my job—to get contracts and car loans purchased. I had a construction background before I got into the auto industry. With that background, plus my negotiating expertise, I decided to invest in a piece of property and flip it, which I really enjoyed. Then I thought, *Why am I giving all this money to a real estate agent?*

I then decided to become one myself and got my real estate license around the time of the recession, *which was a perfect time to learn the business. (Joking)* I did that part time, just trying to figure out my way. *What am I going to do, how am I going to make money?* There were just so many different ways to do it in real estate. A friend gave me a book, *6 Steps to 7 Figures* by Pat Hiban. I read it and it made sense. In that book Pat Hiban talked about two business partners, Tim Rhode and David Osborn. I looked up Tim on Facebook.

Tim retired when he was 40, and I was 41 when I got my real estate license. I sent him a message on Facebook but thought, *This guy's never going to answer me.* But he immediately got back to me. I had written, "Hey, I know you don't know me from Adam, and I'm sure hundreds of people have asked you this, but can I have two minutes on the phone with you?" And he said, "Sure."

I found out Tim Rhode was a coach and told him I wanted what he had. Then I had a conversation with my wife and said, "You're not going to like this, but I'm hiring this gentleman." She said, "I trust you." Boom! Big support. I hired Tim to be my coach, and he helped me put together a plan to become a full-time real estate agent and business owner. That was something I'd wanted to do for a long time, but I didn't have anybody in my life to get advice from or to model myself after. My background was blue-collar construction. I didn't have any multimillionaires or business owners in my life. That seemed too far away. They were on the other side of the railroad tracks.

When I first put together a plan, I told Tim I wanted to become a full-time real estate agent in a year. Tim said six months. That freaked me out, but I did it in four! It turns out I was teachable. At 41 years old I didn't know anything. How would I turn the fantasy of being a business owner into my reality? I didn't have any tools. I didn't have any associations with people. I just did whatever Tim told me to do. I can tell you, be teachable.

The first thing he had me do was to clean up my finances. I'd never learned how to manage money. I'd lived like a drunken sailor my whole life and had four kids and a wife who depended on me. I had to put together a plan for how to set myself up financially. I had to look at what I was good at and I found I was good on the phones.

I needed to learn how to write a goal. I had to be specific, and it had to have a time date on it, otherwise it was just a dream. We put together a one-year plan, a five-year plan, and a 10-year plan. I have a 90-day vision I visualize every morning, and I review my goals at least once a week and make adjustments. I hired an assistant, and she became my consultant, my transaction coordinator, my photographer. She did everything for me, and I paid her per transaction. I just hammered the phones. I was working five days a week at my other job and two days a week doing real estate.

The money started coming in, and I was able pay off my debts. July 11, 2014, I call my freedom day. It's when I walked out of that dealership for the last time. But here's the thing to know: I learned from Tim to write out the story of how this would go down. I put that story together as if it had already happened—exactly what I was going to do, the amount of money I was going to make, how I would feel walking out of the dealership. When the day arrived, it happened just as I'd visualized it. It was surreal. It was the best feeling of my life at the time.

*** 

Philip is a personal hero of mine. His willingness to step into the unknown while simultaneously asking for and then receiving support is a powerful demonstration of self-love, responsibility, and maturity. He didn't leap into the void completely unprepared. He took the risk to ask for help and then took the risk to make the changes his mentor encouraged him to make. He embraced his path with commitment and courage and it paid off!

> *"The biggest risk is not taking any risk....*
>
> *In a world that's changing really quickly,*
>
> *the only strategy that is guaranteed to fail is not taking risks."*
>
> *~ Mark Zuckerberg ~*

**Is It Worth the Risk?**

Always ask yourself that question before contemplating taking a real risk. After all, the definition of risk in the Merriam-Webster online dictionary is "possibility of loss or injury." However, taking a risk at some point in your journey toward your goals is often essential. There are of course smaller risks and bigger risks. There is no reason to take a big risk unless you are willing to bear the potential loss. Taking any risk is a profoundly personal decision and should not be made lightly.

I would never advocate a one-size-fits-all prescription for the degree or kind of risk one should consider taking in order to achieve a goal. But I have included this as a principle for self-transformation because in my experience it is almost impossible to completely avoid taking risks as you move forward in life. On some level, everything can be seen as a risk. You risk rejection when you ask someone to go out with you or to help you. You risk financial loss when you leave one job for another, or a "secure" job to create your own business. You risk failure when you set about learning and applying a new skill.

I can't promise you that you will not be rejected, or that you won't experience loss or failure. But I do know for sure that if you avoid taking risks, you will never have the opportunity to achieve your heartfelt desires. Any dream, any goal, that is true to your heart and soul will require taking risks and will often require taking a big or many big risks. However, it is my belief that failure, rejection, and loss are not bad but simply a part of life. Failure gives us the message that we need to course-correct, or that we have something important to learn or understand that we might not have learned if we hadn't taken the risk and failed. If we stay open to the message in failure, we may discover that "failing" is a gift disguised as pain, fear, or disappointment.

I also believe that because taking a risk is in essence taking a leap of faith, there is something, some energy (God, Source, the Universe, Spirit, a Guardian Angel, Soul, or whatever you want to call it) that meets us when we make that leap of faith. Of course, I can't prove this, but I have over and over in my life been met with what I call Divine

171

support when I have had the courage to put myself out and risk. I think of calculated risk-taking as an affirmation to our Higher Selves (God within or Soul) that we have faith in our dreams and our goals and ultimately in ourselves.

So, ask yourself, "Is it worth the risk?"

## Exercises

For this chapter I offer only one exercise:

1. After you've done the work in the previous chapters on goals and taking action, pick the first action step you listed, the one that is the smallest and most immediate step toward your goal, and take it!

**Remember:** The **O** in **FREEDOM** stands for **Opening** yourself to **Opportunity.**

# Chapter Ten

# Networking

*"The richest people in the world look for and build*

*networks,*

*everyone else looks for work. Marinate on that for a*

*minute."*

*~ Robert T. Kiyosaki ~*

**Philip's Story Continued...**

This is the part of Philip's story in which he addresses the importance of networking and creating a support system. In his words:

Tim Rhode invited me to attend an event for his organization, 1Life Fully Lived, in Reno. At the time I had no clue what it was about other than it was Tim's event, but

I wanted to meet the guy. I'd only talked to him on the phone. I was blown away. All the elders from GoBundance were there: Rock Thomas, Mike McCarthy, Pat Hiban, David Osborn. I was meeting all these successful people, and that's when I got involved in GoBundance and learned the power of association. I learned that I need to be around people who are bigger. I need to be the smallest fish in the fish bowl. These were big fish and at first I felt really inadequate. But I found out that they are the most generous people.

A couple of months later I went to a big event in Squaw Valley with GoBundance and met about 200 millionaires from around the world who are all super generous people. A mentor I'd been following for years was attending, and we spent a couple days together there. I learned we can only keep what we have by giving it away. I got really involved in that organization, and started building my own real estate team.

I have a gratitude team too, and every day we send each other a text message with what we're grateful for. I'm also in a Facebook coaching group where we write out what we're grateful for. I have cultivated a great support system.

I found as I was growing personally and professionally, I was attracting successful, generous people. My circle of friends has decreased, but the quality has increased.

Just seek people out. People are so helpful. All you have to do is ask. That's how I got to where I'm at. Somebody pulled me up. So many people I surround myself with are so willing to help. I reached out to the people I was interested in and they said, "Yes, come join us." Find a mentor, reach out, and start talking to people.

\*\*\*

The message of Philip's story is clear. The last sentence of his piece says it all and bears repeating: "Find a mentor, reach out, and start talking to people."

---

"Who *you spend time with matters.*

*Both healthy and unhealthy habits are contagious.*"

~ *Dr. Daniel Amen,* Change Your Brain, Change Your Life

~

---

**Networking and Creating a Support System**

I've never done anything on my own. There has always been somebody supporting my journey, helping to keep me on my path. I remember when I first started to get books from the prison library. The librarian would do whatever she could to get the books I was interested in reading. She understood that if they weren't available to check out, I would have to figure out how to purchase them. And that was a big deal in prison.

There was a teacher in prison who believed in my dream to be in real estate when I was released. He had a newspaper subscription and let me read his paper every day. I would pore over the business and real estate sections, which gave me a lot of real-world information about the business. In an earlier chapter I told the story of a girlfriend who studied with me day and night to help me pass my real estate exam. Without her help I probably would not be a licensed real estate agent today. All these people believed in my journey, and all these people are partially responsible for the fact that I am an ex-felon with a prosperous career in real estate.

In addition to cultivating relationships in your personal sphere, do some research to find people outside of your sphere. These may be people in your field of interest or in positions to help you get connected with people who might be able to give you support, advice, opportunities, or other connections. Reach out, ask for guidance and feedback. Share your journey, ask for help, and then, in turn, offer to be of assistance. If you are transparent, clear about what you are looking for, and willing to offer your services, advice, and assistance in return, you are more likely to find people willing to go out on a limb for you.

By meeting and being around people who are successful in general and successful in your area of interest in particular, you automatically put yourself in a position to succeed. These people will push you, inspire you, motivate you, and support you in both direct and indirect ways. Their presence in your world will push you to the next level in your life. They may even push you out of your comfort zone, but if they are true supporters, and not naysayers in disguise, they will be there for you, cheering you on as you step into more challenging positions.

The power of connections is key, but if you are someone who is afraid to trust, who may have been burned or betrayed in the past, you will have to pay close attention to your gut feelings about the people you ask for help as well as those you invite into your sphere. The truth is, you don't pick the right people, you feel the right people. How do you do that? Do your research. Google. Get referrals. As best you can, try to find out about the person you're going to be communicating with. Then, when you speak to or meet with the person you feel might be a valuable connection, pay attention to the way that person makes you feel. Do you feel uplifted and encouraged? Excited? Inspired? Or do you feel tired, on edge, or even discouraged or uncomfortable? Use your discernment. Listen, tune in, allow your body and your mind to tell you whether this person is someone you can trust.

We can't talk about making connections, networking, or finding a support network without talking about the importance of social media. It's a vital tool for creating success and moving you closer to your goals. I've had the opportunity to travel across the country and participate in speaking engagements through my social media connections. I posted my story on Facebook, and somebody shared it with somebody else and somebody else shared it with somebody else and somebody else shared it with somebody else.

One day I got a phone call from a guy who said, "Man, I want you to speak at an event I'm coordinating in Philadelphia. Can you fly there? We'll pay for your flight and your hotel." After doing some research, and tuning in to my gut, I said, "Yes. How did you hear about me?" He said, "Someone saw your story on Facebook and they shared it with my friend and my friend shared it with me, and it's inspiring and I want to help you in any way that I can." Awesome! You never know who somebody knows. That's the truth. My advice is that if you use social media, use it in the right way. Use it to attract the kind of attention you want. Rather than being negative or showing photos of yourself partying, post material and images of yourself that are authentic but represent your best, most aspirational self.

Because that's what you want to attract—people who are successful, inspiring, friendly, helpful, connected, and supportive.

Whether or not you're comfortable with social media, consider joining a local networking group or check out various Meetup groups. Making face-to-face social connections is always a positive way to find people to add to your support team. Participate in group activities you enjoy—take a yoga class, go on a group hike or rock-climbing expedition, take a painting or writing class, go to a seminar on a topic related to your area of interest, attend a spiritual service at a church or temple. In other words, actively seek out activities where you might find like-minded people. It doesn't always have to be about your business or your goals. Surround yourself with people you like who are friendly and encouraging, who like you and want to be around you.

Remember, you never know what advice somebody will give you that sticks with you forever. By getting out and participating in different activities in different environments, you will eventually get different results for your life. You will open doors for yourself that you never knew were there.

> *"When you find a possible source of valuable information, such as a speaker or someone who has knowledge specific to your industry, ask for their help. Make an effort to build a relationship with them. It will reap great rewards."*
> ~ *David Osborn and Paul Morris,* Wealth Can't Wait ~

**Real Estate Regulatory Committee**

After I got laid off from the mortgage company, I started looking at all the work I'd done. I'd learned about real estate in general, flipping, wholesale flipping, how to buy and sell real estate, how to finance real estate, and how to use other people's money to purchase properties. I wanted to take the real estate licensing exam, but I was worried about my felony. I'd already tried to get my loan officer's license through the mortgage company and got denied because there's a federal law that says if you've had a felony conviction, you cannot get a license.

I'd been doing a lot of public speaking about legislative bills in Washington State, and the attitude the government has toward people who are or have been incarcerated. At one of these engagements I met someone on the Real Estate Regulatory Committee and thought to myself, *If there's anybody who would be able to tell me if I can get my license, it would be this person.* So I reached out and said, "Hey, I want to get my license. Who would deny me based on my criminal history?"

She told me to send her my information. Soon after, I got a phone call from her saying, off the record, that it was going to be approved but that it was going to take a little bit of time. She told me to go ahead and start taking real estate classes. I started but got lazy and wound up stopping for almost a year. My amazingly supportive girlfriend at the time, as you read about earlier encouraged me to try again. She studied day and night with me. We set a goal on my calendar to have certain chapters done. She made PowerPoint presentations that helped me understand the key terms. So we studied and studied and then I took the test and passed. But I still had to wait to hear whether I would actually get my license as I'd been assured two years earlier.

When I passed the test, I called Ben Kinney, an agent I'd met in a restaurant who knew a little bit about my story.

I said, "Hey, I passed the test and now I'm not sure what to do."

He said, "Get on a plane to Texas. There's a convention you need to be at."

"I'm not sure if you realize...I just got laid off and I only have about $200 in my bank account."

"Just get there. Figure it out."

I figured out how to get there, of course, and was looking around for Ben in this massive hall with at least 15,000 other real estate professionals. Suddenly he came out on stage!! And I thought, *Who is this guy! I met him at a restaurant and here he is talking to 15,000 people.* A couple of days later I was sitting in one of the classes at the convention and my phone buzzed. I had an email from the regulatory committee that said, "Congratulations, you've been approved to get your license." Right there in that moment I became a real estate agent! I started to cry—tears of absolute joy. No joke. It was that emotional. To come from where I did and to go through all I had. To arrive and be there in Texas surrounded by thousands of Realtors who had gone down this journey. And there in that moment I was told that I too was being recognized as a real estate agent just like them. AMAZING!!

> *"Networking is not about just connecting people. It's about connecting people with people, people with ideas, and people with opportunities."* ~ *Michele Jennae* ~

## Kenny Parker's Story

I'm so proud of Kenny. He's been through a lot of tough times and had the courage to finally ask for help, which is why he has this story to tell. His story is so important because it's a testament to the fact that when you are ready to take responsibility for your life and accept help, you will find it. This is a small part of Kenny's story, told in his own words:

I drank and drove. I crashed cars. I stole cars. I did insane stuff when I was drinking. When I was doing drugs, I felt like I was a low risk to society, but probably a higher risk to myself. However, I wasn't really worried about how it affected me. I was battling serious levels of depression and anxiety. The last two or three years I was using, I had a heavy painkiller addiction. Before I started taking painkillers, I don't think I ever felt suicidal, but I was definitely depressed and hated the state of my life.

I spent about two or three years taking painkillers every single day. That was a really expensive habit. Every single night during my final year of addiction, I prayed I wouldn't wake up. When I did wake up, I prayed I would stop living the life I was living. It became a really, really small, depressing life. My friends stopped hanging out with me. My girlfriends were gone. My family didn't care for me. I had nothing going on because the only people I wanted to hang out with and the only people I needed in my life were the people who could help facilitate my addiction.

187

I woke up one morning and realized I had no more money left. I wasn't willing to commit another crime. I wasn't willing to do anything to get the financial means to continue my addiction. I probably only had a couple minutes to pick up the phone and ask for help, because I knew if I stayed in a state of withdrawal for very long, I was going to kill myself. I picked up the phone, called my mom, and said I needed to go into treatment. A massive weight was lifted off my shoulders. I had been wanting to ask for help for years, but didn't have the willingness to do it.

I woke up that morning and I guess, by the grace of God, I had the willingness in that specific moment to pick up the phone and ask for help. I didn't know it, but people were always there for me, just waiting on the other end of the phone, waiting for Kenny to call and say he was done. And as soon as I said I was done, there was a boatload of support.

\*\*\*

As Matthew Kelly, the author of *The Rhythm of Life: Living Every Day with Passion and Purpose,* writes, "The people we surround ourselves with either raise or lower our standards. They either help us to become the best version of ourselves or encourage us to become lesser versions of ourselves. We become like our friends. No man becomes great on his own. No woman becomes great on her own." This quote sums up the lesson to be learned from this part of Kenny's journey. When Kenny was doing drugs, he surrounded himself with the people who would enable his self-destructive drive. When he was ready to make a change, to reset his mind and transform himself and his life, he called for support from the people who loved him. He got the assistance he needed to survive, which in turn, has given him the opportunity to get married and pursue his dreams.

**Support and Encouragement**

It's important to surround yourself with people who believe in your journey, who support and validate your goals and dreams. You need these people to give you encouragement and hold your vision for you, because there will be days that are hard, days when you will doubt yourself and your goals. These are the days when you need a friend, colleague, counselor, teacher, minister, mentor, or family member who is willing to keep you inspired and moving forward when you just want to crawl back into bed. These are the people who will give you the courage to stay on track when you falter or feel you want to give up entirely. This is your support system, and without them it is much harder to stay focused on your personal goals.

> *"If you want one year of prosperity, grow grain. If you want 10 years of prosperity, grow trees. If you want 100 years of prosperity, grow people."* ~ *Chinese Proverb* ~

**Exercises**

Here are some questions and exercises to help you understand how to make connections and create a support system:

1. Look at the goal you settled on and jot down a list of people who might be able to help you get closer to your goal.

2. Now make another list of people who have been a support for you on a personal and professional level, including family, friends, colleagues, employers, employees, and clients. If there are people you don't know well (or at all) but would like to have as a part of your personal support team, add them to your list.

3. Take your first list and choose the one person you feel most intimidated by and the one person you feel you would be most comfortable contacting. Unless you are ready to take a real risk, reach out to the person you feel most comfortable contacting. I recommend either calling or emailing this person (unless you only have access to them through Facebook or LinkedIn—in which case, use

the resources you have) since you will want to give them some information about what you're looking for.

4. Which brings us to what you're looking for. Do you want general advice, connections, access, financial backing, information, or something else? Be sure you are clear about what kind of support you are looking for before you contact this person.

5. In your conversation or email exchange with this person, after you have asked for their assistance, I recommend asking whether there is something you can offer them in return. If this is not appropriate, and if you decide to meet in person, perhaps offer to treat them to coffee or a meal, or bring a small token of your gratitude. This can sometimes be tricky. You don't want to appear to be bribing someone for their assistance, but on the other hand, you want to acknowledge the fact that they may be going out of their way to do something for you. You will have to use your discernment.

6. Now, look at your second list. Pick one person to send a letter (email, Facebook message, text) of gratitude to.

Think about how this person has supported or championed you and acknowledge them.

7. As you move through your list, continue to refine and add if necessary. Make notes about who has helped you and how so you remember to give them credit and thanks.

8. Keep sending notes of thanks to the members of your personal support team and take note of how your relationships grow and develop as you acknowledge them.

9. In addition to your lists, get out and meet strangers. Go to Meetup events in your area. Join networking groups, take classes, go on dates, join a book club or a social group affiliated with a local church or spiritual center. All these activities will give you opportunities to share your dreams and goals and connect you with like-minded people. You never know where your opportunities will come from. Stay open and have fun!

**Remember:** The **M** in **FREEDOM** stands for **Meeting Many** people.

# Epilogue

*"You are here to live, to be happy, and to love."*

~ *Don Miguel Ruiz,* The Four Agreements ~

One morning after I'd been in Jakarta for a week, I woke up from a bad dream. I was still in a lot of pain about the end of my relationship and was questioning my path. I lay there thinking about the direction my life was going in and the people I'd lost. I said to myself, "Well, I can continue to lie here thinking about all this painful stuff or I can start making some moves to get out of it."

I got out of bed, took a shower, and went downstairs to eat breakfast. This particular morning I was happy to see fried potatoes in the buffet, an American breakfast item I hadn't seen on the menu before. I had a few eggs with my potatoes and began to feel much better. Then I met up with my friends David and Mily, and we went to Pasar Baru, a big open-air market in the center of the city that was created around 1820. This amazing market was one of the very best experiences I had in Jakarta.

While wandering around I kept seeing affirmations on doorways, on T-shirts, and even vehicles. I bought a Nike T-shirt with "Just Don't Quit" written across the chest, which made me feel even better than the potatoes from breakfast! We walked by a street vender who was displaying a sea of model cars (over a thousand or so). Immediately my eye went to one model car. The only car like it in the bunch—a white Lamborghini!

I thought, *No way! This is insane.* With all the affirmations I had been seeing that day and now this, I knew the Universe was talking to me! Anybody who knows me well knows that I've wanted a white Lamborghini for as long as I've known what a Lamborghini is. And there it was, my vision, my dream, my goal, or at least the symbol that represents my biggest goal in life. Growing up as poor as I did, I never even imagined a Honda was possible, much less a Lamborghini. Though it is a beautiful and expensive car, it is not the status of the white Lamborghini that attracts me, it is what it represents that makes it a special symbol of my highest aspiration, of the most precious of all of my goals— FREEDOM!

\*\*\*

When I started writing this book, I was asked, "How much money would you like to make with this book?" My reply was, "I'm not concerned about the money; I just want to help one million people change their lives." That is truly my goal with this book. I have been through so much in my short life, and there really hasn't been a roadmap for any of it. I've read so many books by great authors that have helped me get to right where I am in this moment—writing to you from my laptop. They have been my teachers and have helped me figure out these Dedicated 8. I offer them to you through this book since I am not there with you in person to guide you.

You have the power to change your life RIGHT NOW! You can be free of stress, drama, boredom, or whatever's going on in your life that you want to change. Follow this book. Change your mindset. Change your life! No one else can do it but you.

If I was able to survive...

an abusive family environment,

a rough and abusive foster care system,

17 years of prison starting at 14 years old,

And...

achieve freedom,

become a Realtor,

become a speaker,

travel the country,

go to Asia,

become an author,

you can change your life too!

Thank you for reading my book. Please connect with my Facebook page and let me hear your story and support you as you move toward your goals!

# Conclusion

Where you are in this moment reading this is a result of your actions up to this point thus far in your life!

Where you go from here depends on your dedication to res3t yourself and the choices you make from this point forward to live the best life YOU WANT!

Don't wait to move forward any longer to live your best life! Start right now! Start today! You CAN DO IT!

# Res3tConnect

Networking is key for accomplishing your goals! If there is anything I can do to help you on your journey or to add value to your journey, please connect with me.

I would be grateful to connect with those who have read this book or interacted with me in anyway. If you would like to connect directly with me, you can email me at: connect@res3t.com. I look forward to hearing from you and seeing how I can help you on your journey to accomplish your major goals!

**Want to be in real estate?**

A question I frequently get is "how can I become a real estate agent?" I would be happy to help you with your journey and connect you with some amazing people in your area to help you on that path! Email me at realestate@res3t.com and I will be happy to help you!

**Writing a book?**

Writing this book has been a journey. I would be happy to help you with your book writing journey as well. Connect with me at: writeabook@res3t.com and we can see what the win win situation looks like to help you accomplish your goal!

**One request from me**

If you found that this book was helpful to you, helped changed your mindset in any way and you see that Res3t can help take any or every area of your life to the next level, I'm asking that you pass this book along to someone else. Give this book to an awesome person you know. Or if you love it too much to part with it long term, let them borrow it. Or even better, send them their own copy as a gift to let them know they matter to you and that you want to support them in their journey to live their very best life!

My goal is to help a million people. With your help spreading the word my goal can be a reality. Thank you.

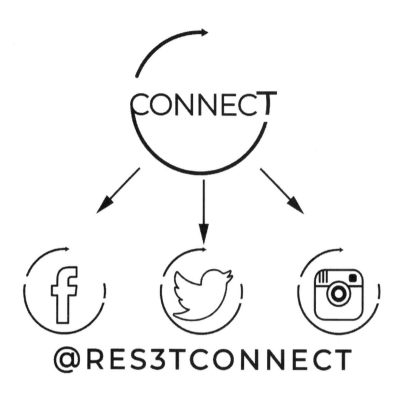

I would love to hear your Res3t stories! Please share your journey with the Res3t community at www.facebook.com/res3tconnect

Connect with Res3t online. To follow me on any platform just go to res3tconnect on that platform!

# Thank You!

*"Without friends no one would choose to live."*

*~ Aristotle ~*

Without the people named here, *Res3t* would never have been written.

I want to thank the **City of Olalla** for being such an amazing place to grow up, and the teachers and administrators at **Olalla Elementary School** for having so much compassion for me and my brother, Bill.

I want to thank my brother, **Bill**, for always being here for me through every struggle and always being the first one to say, "You'll get through this, man. It's just the same shit, different day."

Surviving prison wouldn't have been possible without some core friends. Thank you, **Shane VanGerpen, Dolphy "Blue" Jordan, Big Tom Langbein, Steve McCabe** and **Logan Gore**! To this day, you all inspire me and guide me and lift me up, and I appreciate each one of you and your families.

If it weren't for **Randy Bale**, **Michael Woodhouse**, and **Norm Dauth**, my journey might not have gone as quickly as it did. The three of you stepped away from your comfort zones and worked toward *real change* in a prison and prison system that wasn't familiar with your kind of thinking. You helped change my life, and I appreciate all three of you very much.

**Kym Hanes**, you helped me change my mindset and grow inside prison and out. You were and are positive and encouraging and caring. I appreciate the friendship we have and I'm proud to call you my friend.

**Michael and Mary Tutty**, I am forever grateful for the chance you gave me, and for the bond and friendship we have created since we first met. The world needs more genuine people like you. I could write forever about the two of you. I appreciate you both so very much and I love you both.

I want to thank **Jina McEnany-Fijorick** for always believing in me. If it weren't for you, I would never have become a Realtor. So for that and many other things, I am grateful for the time you were in my life.

**Tim Rhode**, you have blessed my life! You have no idea. I have traveled because of you, I have met people I thought I'd never meet because of you, and I have had many unexpected opportunities because of you. This book exists because of you. Thank you for your friendship—it means a lot to me.

**Hannah Emmings**, **Roy Allen**, and **Jen Young**, I care for all of you and without all that has happened between us, I don't think this book would have ever been written. It started with the statement, "You need to reset yourself." That was the inspiration for the title of this book and the genesis of the book itself. Regardless of how everything ended, I loved and appreciated the journey I had with each one of you.

I want to thank two amazing people I met in Jakarta, Indonesia: **Arty Batari** and **Derya Ulucay**. The two of you helped me grow, accept my life circumstances, and res3t my mindset more than you know. I am very grateful that the two of you came into my life when you did, and I'm excited for our reunion in the USA!

I want to thank **David Taufiq**, my friend and interpreter while in Indonesia. You gave and still give me hope with your positivity, your story, and your love for life. I am very appreciative of you and the friendship we built while I was on this journey. I am excited for your future!

I want to say thank you to **Ben Kinney**—for your friendship, your late-night texts, your guidance, and sometimes even your humor. ☺ You took a chance with me and have been a call or text away through some very serious stuff in my life. I'm endlessly grateful for you!

**Hal Elrod**, you took my phone call and have been supportive and generous with your guidance. Without you this book wouldn't have been born. Thank you for everything!

**Suzanne Potts,** I owe you a lot more than just a thank you. You've been on an incredible journey of your own, side by side with me, and you have championed me and my vision through our many phone calls. I am so impressed by you. You have such admirable strength and wisdom, I can't wait to see what your future holds! Thank you in advance for being in mine!

**Be Phan**, you were in my life during some of my darker days, and you gave me some of the best life advice I've ever gotten, which I carry with me every day: *"Do the right thing every day and you will have a good life."* My gratitude and respect for you and your family is never-ending. I am grateful that you opened the door for me to get to know all of you and that you accepted me.

**Steve and Christine McCabe**, the two of you have been my rocks for so many years now. You have given me a place to think and to res3t multiple times. You have seen smiles, tears, and even a drunk pirate! I love you guys so much. Without you this book couldn't exist

**Walt and Annette Cummings**, I want to thank you both for your love and support and your dedication to our friendship. You have given me so much happiness over the last few years and have brought me around in some dark times. Thank you for the many calls and the drop-everything moments!

I would like to thank **Terry Olson**, who has been my mentor, friend, and pastor. Your guidance has always led me down the right roads, and without your love and support for all these years, none of my accomplishments would have happened. Thank you for every lesson, every sermon, every lunch, and every boat ride. You have had a powerful and positive impact on my life!

I want to also thank **Brooke and Ken Nadeau**. You opened your home up to a stranger and gave me HOPE. Not sure where I would be right now in this moment without the opportunity you gave me. I am forever grateful.

I want to thank **Christina Kyle**. You were more than a rock for me. You were there for me when no one else could be. You were there morning, noon, and night. Because of our conversations I was able to res3t myself multiple times. There are no words that can express how meaningful your friendship during that time was to me.

Finally, I want to thank everyone who gave their time and shared their stories with me to help emphasize the Dedicated 8 throughout this book!

## BRING JEFF TO YOUR EVENT!

Have Jeff give a keynote address at your organization's events, or a motivational speech at your high school, college or university.

Jeff is a top-rated speaker who offers customizable entertaining talks and workshops on the topics of Res3t, leadership, sales, addiction, mindset and goal setting.

To schedule with Jeff email events@res3t.com

## Visit www.Res3t.com

Made in the USA
Lexington, KY
16 October 2018